I Felt Like an Adventure

I FELT LIKE AN ADVENTURE

A Life of Mary Burkett

by

BEN VERINDER

Mary Burkett
18·6·12.

1st.

The Memoir Club

© Ben Verinder 2008

First published in 2008 by
The Memoir Club
Arya House
Langley Park
Durham
DH7 9XE

British Library Cataloguing in
Publication Data.
A catalogue record for this book
is available from the
British Library

ISBN: 978-1-84104-189-6

Typeset by TW Typesetting, Plymouth, Devon
Printed by The Cromwell Press, Trowbridge, Wilts

To David Marshall and
the Reverend Richard Theodosius
with thanks

Contents

List of Illustrations

Acknowledgements

Particular thanks to Valerie Rickerby, whose history of Isel is the source of much of the final chapter and who generously allowed me to quote (extensively) from her work with M.E.B. on Percy Kelly, to Genette Dagtoglou neé Malet de Carteret, whose diaries proved of great assistance when writing the Persia chapter, and to Paul Pollitt, former Isel guide, for proof-reading the first version of the manuscript. Any errors in the text are mine. I am also very grateful to those who took the trouble to send me personal memories of M.E.B. and other biographical information. Not every testimony has appeared in print but all have helped add depth to the portrait. Thanks to Svetlana Alliluyeva, Edward Allington, Dr Doreen Browne, Jonathan Carr, Jenny Cowern, David Cross, Jocelyn Davison, Lady Egremont, Inge Evers, Mrs Graham Greene, Ann Louise Moore, Sophie Nicholls, Olive Rummens, David Sloss, Mary Wane, Josephine Whitehead.

This work would have not been possible without the full assistance of Mary Elizabeth Burkett, who has been most generous with her time, advice and correspondence. With typical tenacity she did not give up on this book, even when I had.

Foreword

By Melvyn Bragg

Children usually get adults right. My three have delighted in Mary Burkett since first they met her years ago. They smile whenever her name is mentioned. They laugh aloud with pleasure recalling their encounters with her. Like me they enjoy the force of her ardent commitments and the singularity of her life.

I think I first met Mary in her wigwam house in the woods several decades ago. The place was a living museum, stockpiled with the evidence of a lifetime of roving – especially in the Middle East, most intensively in Persia. Maybe her remarkable curiosity and quest to uncover ancient civilisations comes from the dramatic mixture of genes – on her mother's side a pedigree reaching back to the Court of Charlemagne, on her father's a remarkable Private in the Royal Engineers when he met his exotic wife.

She had rather a wild childhood and became and remains an autodidact – archaeology, ornithology, felt making, Cumbrian artists, Roman remains . . . the list marches on. It seems to me that Mary has managed to do everything she has wanted to do and from a standing start has ended up living in a beautiful house in Isel in God's own country – the Northern Lake District.

Isel Hall boasts a splendid though stubbornly leaky pele tower.

A major turning point in her life seems to have been the 7½ months' trip to Persia in 1962 with Genette Malet de Carteret, a young lawyer – an Oxford graduate.

Their often alarmingly intrepid expedition recalling similar forays into the unknown by similar English women with a blind faith in their capacity for survival and a justified belief that dollops of good luck would come their way took them to the Turcoman Nomads, an Assassins Castle saw bullet holes slam into their sturdy van, led them to unexplored sites and to multiple brief worrying encounters most of which had a charming resolution.

That was in 1962 and it set Mary on the path to become a regular guide to a spread of countries across the Middle East and in my view gave her rather concealed romantic nature all the nourishment it craved.

She has met and befriended scores of famous people like Freya Stark and little wonder – they are like two peas in a pod. In Cumbria she has become a patron and a friend to many fine local artists – Julian and Linda Cooper, Jenny Cowern, Percy Kelly, besides finding house room at Isel Hall for Josefina de Vasconcellos and Edward Hughes. Through her books and her advocacy she has reinforced the reputations of Sheila Fell, William Green and Mathias Read – to stick only to her local connections and there is rarely a cultural enterprise worth the name in Cumbria which does not consider itself fortunate to have Mary on board. Apart from her zest, her experience as an outstanding director of Abbot Hall makes her someone to be treasured.

A rich subject. Someone who practises plain living and high thinking but has a compelling attraction to the ancient mysteries. So she'll be amused to know that I read this book in Marrakech and am writing this Forward after a visit to its ancient Koranic School. When next I meet her she'll insist I tell her about everything I saw.

And then point out what I missed.

April 2008

CHAPTER 1

Aquitaine Onwards

SHOULD A BIOGRAPHY BEGIN WITH a birth, this book bursting into life between the cold white walls of the Newcastle Royal Infirmary maternity ward on 7 October 1924? Or open at the meeting of biographer and subject on a bright summer day seventy-four years later, a young newspaper reporter stepping into the entrance hall of a Cumbrian castle to meet the owner's outstretched hand?

Neither, says the owner; this story, she suggests, should start with William, favourite of Charlemagne, scourge of the Saracens, captain of the first cohort of the Holy Roman Emperor's guard and protector of Aquitaine (as surrogate for the Overseer, Charlemagne's three-year-old son Louis le Debonair).

Duke William successfully defended Aquitaine against those Saracens, recaptured Orange and paid compliment to the Greeks and Ali Baba in his daring assault on Nîmes – entering the city disguised as a merchant, his troops packed in barrels for a surprise attack. 'Even his defeats added to his prestige and furnished fresh tales of his power and prudence,' wrote family historian Alice Gaussen. 'Like the heroes of Homer he did not fear to run away. "Believe me," he told an impetuous nephew, "retreat when necessary and return to the charge and never wait for death. Flight is good if it saves the body."'

In 804 William, body saved but soul weary, retired from martial life and ordered a church to be built in the mountains near Verdun at Gellone. Two years later, dressed in a goat's hair shirt and carrying a supposed shard of the true cross (presented to him by Charlemagne in recognition of his service to the Emperor), he turned away from his family, war and politics, and marched alone up to Gellone. After six years of prayer and solitude, Saint William of the Desert (as he became known after his beatification) died.

Among those he left behind was his son Gausselin – from whom Mary Burkett's maternal family take their name. The Gaussens' genealogical tree sags with the breathless titles of French aristocracy, from Raimond Gausselin, Seigneur de Sabran et d'Uzes, to Bernard,

1

Bishop of Béziers and Archbishop of Narbonne. By the tenth century the family had become an important force in the south of France. Crusaders and lords of Languedoc, they minted their own coins, kept their own courts and built sturdy chateaux beside vast hunting forests. Fortune favoured the family until the sixteenth century, when the Inquisition abruptly interrupted the Gaussen *bonne chance*. As Protestants threatened with the auto-da-fé, they fled France, dispatching grateful prayers from the Huguenot pews of England and Ireland.

It was from Ireland that Mary's maternal grandmother Mary Ellen Gaussen, an austere woman shepherding four precocious daughters, began her own peregrinations after the death of her husband James in 1896. The family moved to Brussels, where they enjoyed the mussels and the exchange rate, then on to Bournemouth in 1905, Ireland and finally Paris. When they were not packing cases the sisters delighted in music and they formed a quartet: Sasie, the eldest, played the piano, Mary's mother Alice the violin and Barbara the cello. Maude sang.

Clergy collect on the lower boughs of the Gaussen tree. James Gaussen had been a parson; the Bishop of Ripon was a first cousin, another cousin a Dean. Sasie – tall, elegant and a committed Christian – chose the missionary path. In 1905, despite family protests, she arrived in Fukien, south-east China, to begin her life's work as schoolteacher and missionary. Throughout her childhood Mary would receive rice paper letters from this exotic aunt, some crackling with stories of the peasants Sasie had befriended – including the family who served her roast rat and, when their English guest politely declined a second helping, insisted she take it since 'it was caught in the very best room of the house' – and others fraught with desperation and danger.

'Here, after nearly four years of blockade and bombing we know what war means,' Sasie wrote to Mary from a missionary home for blind children near Foochow on 20 April 1941, as the Japanese invaders swept across the country. 'The thousands who died in Foochow alone from starvation – the people one meets looking thin and haggard. Except bloated profiteers, those hoarding rice until the price rises twenty or *forty* times what it should – or, people who steal and sell other people's boys to the enemy – and rice!

'Yesterday we had planes over us all day, and heard bombs drop down the river. Today, we are not going out at all, by Bishop's orders, as the Japanese are *in* Foochow, they say – and we do not know quite what it will mean to be "occupied" . . .

'I have great difficulty in feeding a little family here – a very crippled "old girl" of our blind school in Kienow [where Sasie worked before the war and later returned], married to a blind boy, and their little child Peter – such a helpless starving family.'

Sasie survived the war but did not have much time to enjoy the peace; in 1950 she contracted tuberculosis. Carried fifty miles on a stretcher to an airfield by Chinese friends, she was flown to Ireland and then the south of France, where she died. A plaque in Salisbury Cathedral commemorates her work.

Aunt Barbara's war was similarly dramatic. A citizen of Paris in 1940, the flaxen-haired student of Jung made an unorthodox escape when the Germans invaded the country. Her mother, perhaps too old to summon the energy for one more flight, had died in the French capital shortly after the collapse of the Maginot Line. As the Germans advanced, Barbara packed her belongings into the attic of the Gaussen house before pedalling south on a borrowed bicycle, accompanied by the family dog. Bombed and strafed by the Luftwaffe, ducking under cover as planes dived towards her, the verges littered with dead bodies, Barbara finally reached the coast, where she found a boat to take her to England. She had to leave the dog and the bicycle behind.

After hiding from a German convoy in the Channel, Barbara reached home and almost immediately joined the Red Cross. Soon she was working in-country with the Free French. She survived the conflict but never spoke to Mary of her work with the resistance and unfortunately no written record of her wartime escapades exists.

Aunt Maude the singer chose a more sedate, scholarly path, becoming the first woman to receive a degree from Trinity College, Dublin and marrying Book of Kells expert (and fervent Irish Nationalist) Frank Stephens.

Mary's mother Alice met Ridley Burkett in Bournemouth shortly after the outbreak of the First World War. He was a Royal Engineers private preparing for dispatch to France. She was a violinist entertaining troops at a 'soldiers' home' evening. Romance blossomed but would take time to achieve full bloom. Alice, an elegant young lady with long red hair tucked in a neat bun, was an aristocratic specimen; Ridley Burkett was not. Grandmother Gaussen was slow to bless the union.

Love lasted in the letters between sweetheart and soldier despite a long separation and Alice and Ridley married in France after the Armistice, finally settling in Ridley's native Newcastle upon Tyne. Mary was born in the city on 7 October 1924 and, while Alice nursed her child, Ridley launched a peripatetic career making and repairing watches and occasionally designing scientific instruments. An often unconventional man, Ridley had little interest in a nine to five existence, preferring to spend his days digging in the garden, watch work relegated to the night hours, when he could be found in the basement, curled over a bench, a magnifying glass to his eye.

Similarly unconventional was Alice and Ridley's decision to send Mary to live with her grandmother in Northern Ireland when she was just 18-months-old. 'People sometimes tell me it was unkind – what my mother did, abandoning me – but I never thought so,' says Mary. 'She just thought I would be better off in Ireland and she had another baby [Mary's sister Josephine] on the way and would have found it difficult to manage.'

Her new home was a grand house on the Antrim coast called Tober Patrick, replete with parapets and spiral staircase, home to her sombre grandmother. Although she was very young Mary, remembers playing in the kitchen garden with her little Irish terrier, Paddy, watching waves from the Irish Sea wash over the wall during stormy weather and, barred from the house by a truculent cook called Bella, seeking solace in the parsley patch.

By the time she returned to England her parents had moved to the village of Whickham, County Durham, a blend of the bucolic and the industrial. From Mary and Josephine's bedroom window they could see the long row of small miners' houses, and opposite the golden corn waving in the wind, the green hedges stretching over the hillside and the horses slowly dragging their ploughs across distant fields.

Their own garden was large enough for Ridley to grow a good harvest of fruit and vegetables – a prudent pastime, since his horological career would never make them rich; the girls grew up wearing cast-off clothes (and shoes) from well-heeled relations, the Bellinghams; holidays were often in the gift of Ridley's brother Ernest and sister-in-law Jane, who took Mary and Josephine on seaside jaunts in their box-shaped Trojan, or of wealthy Whickhamite Jessica Thompson, who once drove the family to Bamburgh and

Seahouses in her glamorous Rolls-Royce (and presented the girls with a parcel of presents each Christmas).

Mary may not have always deserved such generosity. She was bold and at times elfishly mischievous: spanked for fighting with two young local boys; in disgrace for scribbling on the newly painted house of a Southampton friend; the cause of panic when, on her return from Ireland, she disappeared to find the Captain's cabin, her mother imagining that she had fallen overboard; Alice mortified again when Mary leant out of her pram, pointed to a curate in a long black cassock and shouted,

'Hasn't he got a nice new dress?'

Mary's natural boldness and spirit of adventure would serve her well in later life. Sometimes waywardness was warranted. Alice, worried that her daughters would grow up talking with a Whickham accent, discouraged the girls from speaking to the local children. They retaliated by mastering a thick Geordie twang when alone together. Nor was it singular – rebellion a trait Mary had evidently inherited from the eccentric Ridley who, under cover of one dark northern night, transplanted a border of flowers from the verdant grounds of an unpopular but affluent Whickhamite to the garden of a poor and friendly neighbour.

Alice's pastimes were more orthodox. Her love of music constant despite separation from the sisters' quartet, she played violin with the Northumbria Orchestral Society once every week, Mary and Josephine listening eagerly for the latch to lift and signal her safe return from Newcastle city. In true Gaussen spirit Alice was a practising Christian; the family stepped through the lich-gate of Whickham's Norman church three times on Sundays. Alice and the vicar, one Marcus Huthwaite (who Mary remembers looked like a medieval monk) became good friends; two intellectuals stranded in a mining town, they shared a mutual passion for butterflies.

At Whickham School Mary's best friend was Billy Hetherington and together they wrote an essay about a fantastic journey to Russia, using bizarre place names gleaned from an old map to lend an air of realism to the tale, for which they won a prize. Outside the classroom Mary became besotted with ornithology and archaeology, Alice and her daughters striding out from Whickham at weekends towards the grounds of Gibside stately home, where the sisters would sit among the golden ferns and listen to birdsong as their mother hunted for

archaeological treasures. Mary also learnt how to climb trees with one
handhold and one good foothold, while the more timid Josephine
helped mother with the housework.

Mary preferred trains, cars and mechanical toys to Josephine's dolls.
Stamps were another early passion. Mary studied watermarks,
counted perforations, examined the different prints. With a family
spread across the globe, exotic stamps bearing elephants, mountains,
bamboo plains or golden statues tumbled through the letterbox to
feed the fires of her imagination. She bound exercise books with
crêpe paper to make albums, subscribed to stamp magazines and
eagerly hunted for flaws.

Josephine recalls Mary's philatelic passions clearly:

'She was always reading at home, answering adverts in newspapers,
sending away for stamps on approval and saving up her pocket money
for weeks to buy a Penny Black, seen in a stamp shop window, and
bought eventually. It was her greatest pride and we looked at it with
reverence.

'Her stamp collection was immaculate and set out so correctly and
neatly. She took a pride in everything she did and designated me as
her "secretary", so of course every task required was gladly done, the
beginnings of the skilful art of delegation, now perfected.'

Alice heard on the radio that Great Britain had declared war on
Germany. She ran out into the street where her daughters were
playing tennis and explained the unhappy news. Industrial Newcastle
and the Tyne valley, Alice and Ridley realised, were likely Luftwaffe
targets; the German bombers would soon be heading for the
shipyards and munitions factories at nearby Elswick. The couple
made plans to send the girls to America, where they would live with
a friend of their mother, but the scheme was quickly abandoned
when Mary and Josephine were told to evacuate to Holwick Hall in
Middleton, Teesdale, alongside their schoolfriends.

Holwick Hall, a shooting lodge owned by the Queen Mother's
Bowes-Lyons family, was paradise to Mary. She would spend whole
days horse-riding among the hills, enjoy epic games of cricket and
rounders, embark upon illicit expeditions to the nearby lead mines to
hunt out bright ores and semi-precious rocks in order to satisfy her
new-found passion for geology. The war years, as Mary describes
them, provide the frame for a girls-own adventure. When the

students weren't sliding down the banisters or listening to the thud of jettisoned bombs burying themselves in the wet grounds, they were creeping out of their dorm windows to follow a distant flashing light across snow-covered lawns, an imagined German spy unmasked as a Teesdale man meandering home from the pub. There are other wartime memories: skirting the school in the dark, checking the blackout windows; the headmistress appointing Mary Head Girl 'to keep her out of mischief'; an unlikely affair between the milkman, brother to three famous singing sisters, and a teacher; Latin taken by correspondence course because the tutor had disappeared in the move to Middleton.

Mary would need the Latin for the General Arts degree she was to read at St Hild's College in Durham, her destination after a summer visiting friends and relatives on both sides of the Irish border. She remembers herself as a green cousin in the Emerald Isle, desperately shy, fluttering between ancestral homes with her sister, the girls' first host Ralph Cope, the charming aged squire of Drumilly, a vast Armagh home whose colossal conservatory Alice had nicknamed The Bubble. Mary and Josephine spent several gentle days rowing across the lake or reading peacefully in their room as a serene Siamese cat stalked through the garden. Then they moved on to Dunany House, home to the Bellingham cousins.

Life with the Bellinghams offered the sisters a close, if uncomfortable, view of the Anglo-Irish aristocracy. The family struggled to recapture their ancestral castle from the undergrowth. The girls' fellow guests, an Admiral and his family, were dauntingly dressed, elocuted, educated and accomplished on the tennis court. Breakfast appeared as a formidable trial of silver-topped serving dishes and unfamiliar etiquette. Invisible servants patrolled the corridors searching for unpolished shoes. The girls were driven to long parties in draughty castles where dashing young servicemen courted countesses.

These were unfamiliar scenes and the girls imagined themselves to be socially ill-equipped. Each morning they listened for the tap of the postman's shoes across the cobbled courtyard, longing for a letter from mother. Eventually the pressure of public 'performance' grew so strong they decided to escape, sent a telegram to their first cousins in Dublin saying they would be arriving earlier than expected, waved goodbye to the Bellinghams and boarded the train, towards a more informal and familiar family.

Mary joined the girls of St Hild's in the autumn of 1942. There were new opportunities for mischief: Mary and friends mimicking the whirr of the air raid siren with such success that their landlady, the friendly Mrs Kirk, spent the night in her shelter; the girls, dressed in their gowns, standing in a line outside Marks and Spencer's pretending to queue for oranges until a trail of expectant shoppers snaked along the pavement behind them, mouths watering at the rare (rationed) exotica, as Mary and the others peeled back to college, leaving a street dreaming of fantastic fruit.

There was time too for new 'passions'. Mary took up photography, snapping the Elvet Bridge, Durham's magnificent cathedral and the swans on the frozen River Wear, developing the photographs in her college digs. She was good enough to catch the attention of the local newspaper picture editor, who bought several prints for the grand sum of one pound per shot. She played the organ in chapel, started rowing (and promptly stopped when the coach told her it would give her a pot belly), improved her painting under the tutelage of a Miss Peddleston (nicknamed Peddles) and joined the rather deceptively titled Adventurers Club, a voluntary community group whose tasks included scrubbing down a filthy sailors' home in Middlesborough, inspected by a curious monkey, and sorting through a warehouse of rotting, maggot-infested wool. Back in Durham she explored the cathedral, home of Bede's tomb, took tea with the charming canon Dr Pace and the marvellously-monikered Headley Spark, held prayer sessions for the Student Christian Movement in the small Galilee chapel (because Aunt Sasie would have approved) and on Sundays visited the redoubtable Miss Tristrams, two missionary friends of Sasie's whose house was a delight of oriental treasures, photographs from India and China, old sandalwood boxes and ornate carvings.

Somehow she found the time to study and graduated with a pass for her General Degree.

During her childhood Mary had wanted to be first a spy and then a detective. Ridley disagreed. He said she would become a teacher. He was right. When Mary finished her degree she began a year's teaching practice in Durham and embarked upon a blackboard career. She took an initial post at St Vincent's, a small school in Alverstoke near Portsmouth, but after an unsatisfying year moved again, this time to a girls' public school called The Laurels at Wroxall Abbey in Warwickshire. Her head was the 'inspirational and inimitable'

Katherine Harvie, who drove an open-topped Grey Shadow and was nicknamed The Saint. Harvie conducted the job interview with Mary across a picnic blanket in a remote country field, having vaulted a five-bar gate.

Mary was initially engaged to teach art at The Laurels but was soon asked to add maths and French to her rota. Retired anaesthetist Doreen Browne remembers her classes well:

'She was very young when she came and so she was only just a little older than some of the senior girls in the school. As a result of her vivacious and friendly personality she became a good friend and confidante of many of the pupils.'

Dr Browne, who was determined to become a doctor but struggled with the requisite mathematics to qualify for a university course, feels that she has particular reason to be grateful to Mary.

'By this time I had been given up by the official maths teacher and the Headmistress as hopeless,' she adds. 'Mary, however, gallantly undertook to take me on, and as a result of her patience and illuminating teaching skills, I managed to pass this subject in 1950 at the last chance before the whole examination system changed. It was a most noble effort on her behalf and typical of her kindness and generosity of spirit.'

It did not take long for Mary to enthuse other students – some Mary in miniature – with her various passions. Granted 'enviable' freedom by Harvie, she camped in the garden with children so that they might listen to the dawn chorus and lead groups of girls on long rambles across muddy fields and through nearby woods. She organised a camera club, encouraging her charges to photograph birds from hides, and turned the old school wine cellars into a dark room. She formed a stamp-collecting club for the youngest class, the diminutive philatelists meeting every Saturday night.

In some pursuits she did not wish to be imitated. At the Warwick branch of Barclays Bank a young teller called Bob persuaded her to tender her telephone number. They began dating each Wednesday and later (to the presumed disappointment of the young stamp collectors) on Saturday evenings. Bob would take Mary to see the Royal Shakespeare Company perform at Stratford. The relationship did not last beyond the RSC season.

Bob was not Mary's first beau; she had met a Navy officer while working at St Vincent's, but his promise of a life in Portsmouth playing his beloved golf did not win her round. A boyfriend at college terrified her by declaring that they 'would have four boys'. In Warwick another admirer took her to see the house he wanted them to share and promptly scared her away.

'I have never met a man I wanted to marry,' Mary explains. She has been in love, she says, with a married man when she was 16 years old. 'Or maybe it was just a crush. Never ever have I felt I really wanted to get married to anybody. By that time I was getting into my career and I remember thinking – I'm not a housewife. Marriage would have certainly meant giving up my career.

'I'm not really the marrying type. When I got old enough to think it out I didn't really want to be sitting in the house all day . . . it was a choice between domestication and a career. I don't regret the choice at all. The only convenience would be now somebody would be here to look after me. I wanted kids when I was a teenager.'

CHAPTER 2

France

SHORTLY AFTER THE END OF the war Aunt Barbara married a former resistance fighter called Omer Baras and they settled in the tiny Catalonian village of Rodès, east of the town of Prades. Rodès, huddled beneath the Pyrenean mountains, was fed by wild tracks and a single dusty road, a primitive place caught in the cycle of mountain life, commanded by the daily ritual of leading goats to pasture. Olive trees, gnarled branches twisting towards the hot sun, lined the steep hillsides. The dry grass sang with crickets and the smell of wild thyme gathered in the evening air. The main street was a gauntlet of cobbles and goat droppings, of old women sitting in the shade on homemade stools, their black shawls huddled in a conspiracy of gossip.

With the war's end Mary's parents accepted Barbara and Omer's invitation to join them, Ridley now retired, Alice happy to leave the cloudy skies of northern England for the Catalonian sun. The two couples shared the same house while another was built for Ridley and Alice further along the village, a home for Mary during her university holidays. She spent many happy days in Rodès Domanova, walking, painting and bird-watching.

She spent time too searching for sites of archaeological interest – a prelude to her Persian adventures – and discovered early on that antiquarianism possesses its own dangers; scratching through the ruins of a castle above the village Mary was stung on the finger by a grey scorpion. She hurried down to Rodès, where a conspiracy of grandmothers warned her that her entire body would soon be pricked by pins and needles. Paralysis would follow, then death. Stung into a panic by this dreadful news she rushed home, announcing that she must see the local doctor for a life-saving injection, brushing aside Alice's protestations and the unpleasant knowledge that a visit to his surgery meant a five-kilometre bicycle ride along hot mountain roads that twisted up and down steep inclines. When Mary arrived, panting and sweating, the doctor agreed to inject her even though, he argued, it didn't sound a very dangerous type of scorpion. The antidote would probably hurt her more than the sting, he said. Again Mary

11

insisted, took the shot and paid her money. She was already feeling queasy halfway through the ride home and for the following few days was confined to bed, as stiff as a board.

The scorpion did little to deter her from amateur zoology – yet another budding pastime. When Mary discovered a praying mantis in a garden peach tree she fed it every day from a teaspoon of milk, fascinated by its ability to mesmerise other animals, transfixing flies with its long swaying forearms. She determined to take it back to England with her for the new term and from the entomologist Fabre learnt how the female of the species eats her partner after courtship (starting with his head), how Egyptians used praying mantis to foretell the sex of a child, and how the Chinese revered them as soothsayers. Her milk-loving mantis lived up to its wise reputation. On the day she was to depart after a summer's worth of teaspoons, she crept into the garden intending to capture it. It had disappeared. (Mary did eventually bring another to England – caught on Avignon station, where she offended the restaurateur by asking if he had any flies to feed it. The new pet survived for six months only, ill suited to the northern climate, despite having a spare room all to itself.)

Mary's contact with the human inhabitants of the Pyrenees was at times equally melancholic. She befriended a young sickly boy called François Villalte, who longed to express the love he felt for his mountainous homeland on canvas and begged Mary to teach him to paint. She agreed but soon the tuberculous François became too ill to meet her for lessons among the olive trees. Gradually she saw less and less of him and one day she was told he had died. As the owner of the only camera for many miles she was asked to photograph the body, according to the Catalan custom. She felt she could not refuse and duly took a picture of the boy laid out in his suit, surrounded by wailing family in a darkened room. It was a harrowing moment for Mary.

This south-west corner of France was a popular spot for famous artists. Among them was the acclaimed Camille Descossy, painter and lecturer at Montpellier University, who had converted a tiny chapel near Rodès Domanova into a house and studio. 'A good-looking, marvellous man,' says Mary, he invited her to visit the chapel during one of his appearances on the main street.

In nearby Prades lived Pablo Casals (known as Pau to his Catalan brethren), the famous cellist. When he practised, beautiful music floated down the street past the queues in the baker's and the bank. Casals, arguably the greatest cellist of the twentieth century, left his native Spain in 1939 in protest at the Franco regime. Georges Bidault, conferring the Legion of Honour upon Casals in 1945, called him 'one of the voices of the world's conscience'. For all his talent (he developed new methods for fingering and bow work, and was an accomplished pianist and composer), he was a modest man. Two years before his death a reporter asked him,

'Mr Casals, you are 95 and the greatest cellist that ever lived. Why do you still practise six hours a day?'

'Because I think I'm making progress,' he replied.

Between 1950 and 1956 Casals organized the Prades music festival, an event still running today. He invited famous musicians like the pianist Eugene Istomin and the violin virtuoso Yehudi Menuhin to play in Prades's church, the festival venue. Mary attended every concert she could, listening out at the close of each evening for his signature tune: The Song of the Birds.

Many French Catalans did not quite appreciate real birdsong in the same way as ornithologist Mary – they cut it short with a shotgun. Hunting was a local passion and to Mary it seemed as if anything feathered was game, including robins and thrushes, on any day of the year.

'It really spoilt my bird-watching,' she says. 'It was as if the people there had no sensitivity. They were interested in their vines, their money, their food, their wine, but, apart from the few who were very cultured Catalans, they were very disappointing people. I always felt they didn't deserve their wonderful land.'

Alice was now suffering from sciatica – aggravated by her regular excursions into the mountains surrounding Rodès – so she moved south with Ridley to the coast at Canet Plage, hoping the Mediterranean waters would help ease her back pain.

One day, swimming alongside her, Mary began to panic – the tide had suddenly swept the pair far out to sea. They waved towards the beach but were too far out to be seen. Mother and daughter paddled towards the shore but the current bore against them; it was as if they were swimming on the spot. Alice cried out that she couldn't make it – Mary should swim on alone. With one last effort she grabbed her mother's hand and started to swim strongly towards shore again. Suddenly her feet touched a sandbank. They were able to stand and rest for a few minutes. It made 'all the difference' and they eventually reached the beach. 'It was one of the worst experiences of my life,' says Mary emphatically.

On one visit to France Mary forged a very influential friendship. At the Protestant church in Perpignan, serviced by a priest who would visit from Marseilles once a year, she met Patrick and Mary O'Brian. The O'Brians were setting up life together in the foothills of the Pyrenees, surrounded by lemon trees and rich vines. They had begun to cut away at the rocks to build a small house, living in a tiny flat on the Rue Arago in Collioure in the meantime.

O'Brian was to become the celebrated author of the Aubrey-Maturin novels set amid the British Navy during the Napoleonic Wars. The series sold millions of copies around the world and made O'Brian that rarity among writers – rich during his lifetime. He was also the biographer of Picasso and Sir Joseph Banks and a translator of many French works. His fans included Tom Stoppard, Iris Murdoch and Charlton Heston. Until his death in January 1999, which triggered a broadside of broadsheet obituaries, he continued to live in the Pyrenean haven he and his wife hacked out from that hillside. Mary O'Brian, formerly married to London divorce barrister Dmitri Tolstoy and mother of historian Nikolai Tolstoy, acted as his editor and typist until her death in 1998.

Collioure was a fitting spot for a writer on maritime matters, having been the port city for Perpignan in the Middle Ages, soaked in the bitter oils of the anchovy trade, its streets once busy with wet coopers, rope-makers, salters and cork cutters. The fauvist art movement was born here, at the hands of Matisse, Derain, Dufy and Marquet; the painters were attracted to the red fields and the acid green vines, the small bleached houses, the church of Notre-Dame-des-Anges and the Chateau Royal, designed by Louis XIV's architectural genius and military engineer, Vauban. Mary recalls the deep blue of the sea there and the beautiful pink of the rooftops, grey and yellow stones, the Chateau Royal jutting out into the bay. And she remembers the O'Brians.

'We were devoted to each other, all three,' she says. 'They didn't have a car at first and they were very poor but we became great friends and it was one of the happiest friendships I have ever had, I think. I looked up to them. They were certainly not my peers, but it didn't seem like that because we got on so well. We were so happy. Mary used to confide in me a lot.'

O'Brian proved himself a loyal friend – at first. In 1953 Mary invited some of The Laurels' girls to the south of France. The party stayed in the Chateau at Collioure, then used as a youth hostel. As the holiday came to an end, France was crippled by a general strike; the rail, post and telephone networks were shut down. O'Brian gathered up some of the students in his car and drove across the border into Spain with the addresses and telephone numbers of every pupil in the party; their parents had to be told that they'd be a week late returning home. On another occasion he invited Mary and some of the girls to take supper at his flat and spent a good part of the evening plucking sea urchin spikes from their legs; Mary and several of the girls had decided to swim to his home from the castle, clambering over rocks in the dark and impaling themselves on the black spines.

Mary would often visit the O'Brians in the small Collioure flat, curling in a sleeping bag on the floor while they snoozed on a big iron bed above her, and later at the house they built and named Correch d'en Baus. O'Brian was just launching his writing career, working on *Testimonies* and *Catalans* during Mary's visits. Despite his ambition, marked by his fastidious writing regime, he was yet to enjoy commercial success. His wife, who Mary says was 'adored' by the Catalans at Collioure, was given spare bread by shopkeepers because the pair was so poor. They grew lettuce, spinach-beet, peas, haricots and potatoes in the garden to save money. 'We are utterly, hopelessly broke, but very cheerful indeed,' Mary O'Brian once wrote to her namesake.

When Mary returned to England she would deliver packages for the couple and wait eagerly for letters from Mary O'Brian describing Patrick's progress, celebrating the reviews of his short story collections, relating the reactions of publishers or her efforts to transform his longhand into type. By return post Mary would send the pair presents of items that were impossible to find in Collioure – a small lamp or a pair of gloves to protect O'Brian's hands from bees and rough cement.

They appreciated Mary's help – the Correch d'en Baus project was tough. Mary O'Brian fell backwards from scaffolding into a pile of sand, and suffered bad bruises. The couple had to work throughout the day and sometimes under moonlight when the delivery lorries arrived with sand, lime, cement and concrete, so that there would be space for fresh loads.

'I despair of *ever* being straight again, so will you please come and see us in spite of dust, dynamite, wounded legs, nowhere to sleep, nothing to eat?' pleaded Mary O'Brian. 'The only thing we can promise you is a great welcome because we are longing to see you . . . We are always up by 6.30 now.'

The run of bad luck continued – Mary O'Brian was stung by a jellyfish on her wrist and developed 'great swollen weals' and in April 1957 she was bedridden with bronchitis. In October that same year she wrote:

'I meant to write ages ago, but we had friends and lately we both had Asian flu and life has been at a very low ebb.'

It was one of the last letters she would write to Mary – the friendship died as suddenly as it had begun. It was an odd expiration: O'Brian had asked Mary to bring a radio set with her the next time that she visited France and had given her the money to buy it. Mary would be working in Austria before travelling down to the coast so she gave the radio to O'Brian's stepson Nikolai to deliver to Collioure. O'Brian was furious and immediately cut off all contact; Mary believes he was angry because the radio had arrived in August, a month later than he had anticipated, and he had missed a particular programme featuring Iris Murdoch, a woman he greatly admired.

Mary tried to apologise, pleading with Mary O'Brian to make her husband change his mind, but was told it was useless. O'Brian simply did not want to be friends any longer. Mary was shocked by this reaction and particularly upset to lose Mary O'Brian's friendship.

'She was fabulous, delightful looking and great fun. She was one of those people you were so delighted to have met. And it just stopped like that. It was the first crushing blow of my life. It really affected me quite hard. I was very upset.'

This seems a conspicuously innocuous event to bring a close friendship to such an abrupt end. It appears as particularly ungracious behaviour on O'Brian's behalf, given Mary's generosity: sending two pairs of gloves for Patrick to wear when building, arranging delivery of the lamp, lending them her telescope, passing on photographs, posting seeds for their garden or bringing hampers of food to their house.

1. St Guillaume, sarcophagus

2. Mother (Alice) and Aunt Sae (Sasie)

3. Aunt Sae and a Chinese family

4. 'Paddy' the dog and Mary at Tober Patrick, Northern Ireland

5. Mary at MacGilligan's Sands, Northern Ireland

6. Ridley Burkett, Mary's father

7. Mary and Josephine at Gibside

8. Tober Patrick, Northern Ireland

9. Mary with a bird-in-hand, Southern France

10. Mary and Una Hall

11. Mary with fellow Durham Students

12. Josephine, Mary's sister, as a student

13. *Holwick Hall*

14. *Katherine Harvie (The Saint), The Laurels School*

15. Mother and Libby Fothergill, Rodès, France

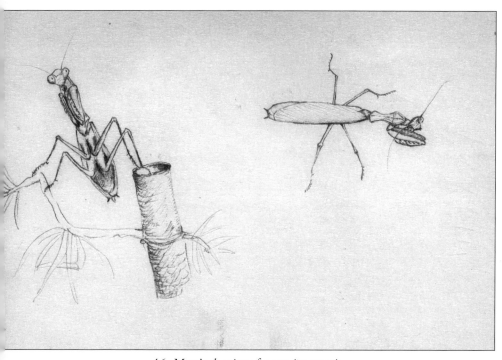

16. Mary's drawing of a praying mantis

17 Sazil hasbahçe

18. Mother and Mary at Canet Plage

19. Patrick O'Brian

20. Collioure

21. Howard Somervell

22. Ockenden Venture house at Millans Park, Ambleside, with co-founder Joyce Pearce in the front row

23. Ockenden Venture home at Millans Park with Mr and Mrs Lovell, housewardens

24. Genette Malet de Carteret

25. Land-Rover, Jersey and Ambleside Expedition to Lakes Van and Urmia, 18 March 1962

26. Girdkuh, Assassins Castle

27. Cannonball Valley, Girdkuh

28. Gunbad-i-Qabus, Iran: King Gunbad's tower mausoleum

29. Gunbad-i-Qabus: first sight of feltmaking

The newspaper articles that followed O'Brian's death offer a clue as to why the writer acted so abruptly. He is described as a man with a ferocious temper who, surrounding himself with fawning admirals and politicians in London's most exclusive clubs, was something of a snob. Indeed Mary O'Brian gives clues to her husband's irascibility in her letters to Mary. Patrick was making himself 'invisible' because a great new work was beginning. The telescope Mary lent them had charmed Patrick 'who does need charming just now'.

Dean King, in his biography of the writer, also suggests that O'Brian's greatest work of fiction may have been his own life. After his death, aged 85, it emerged that O'Brian was not the Irish-born gentleman, accomplished sailor and scholar he had claimed to be. He was actually English and his real name was Richard Patrick Russ. He was born in a large house called Walden, between Chalfont St Peter and Gerrards Cross in Buckinghamshire, on 12 December 1914. His father Charles was the fourth of thirteen children by Karl Russ, an émigré furrier from Leipzig, who had arrived penniless in London in 1862 and had subsequently made a fortune by his death in 1893. Charles became a doctor, specialising in an unpromising method of curing venereal disease, and raised a large family with his adoring wife, Jessie. Patrick was a sickly child when Jessie died of tuberculosis in 1918, just after the birth of their ninth child, Joan. Her death devastated the family and Charles became cold and aloof with his children.

As a boy, O'Brian later claimed, he had taken up sailing and later became quite skilled on the open seas. His son Richard says that is a lie. He also suggested he had been to prep school in Torbay and studied in Dublin, Oxford and the Sorbonne. In fact, he had been mostly tutored at home and finished his education at 14. Dean King reveals that in 1936 O'Brian married Sarah Elizabeth Jones, who was four months pregnant with Richard. Their second child – Jane – was born with spina bifida. After four years O'Brian left his wife and children to fend for themselves in their small Norfolk cottage. He only spoke to Sarah one more time. She told him she hoped he'd rot in hell. He never mentioned the marriage, says King, even to close friends.

In 1940, writes King, O'Brian became an ambulance driver in London where he met Mary, then Countess Tolstoy Miloslavska, and in 1945 they married at Chelsea registry office. Soon afterwards they changed their name by deed poll and went to live in Snowdonia. The Irish persona, says King, was probably developed to ingratiate the couple with the people of Wales who were not well disposed to the English. As for his other lies, he may have been trying to distance himself from a painful childhood. Or, more likely, he was ashamed at how he had treated his wife and children and wanted to rewrite his younger self, to start with a clean page.

'I think he just didn't want to be himself,' says Mary. 'He wanted to make everything completely different, to cover up somehow, because he had had what was rather a disastrous episode leaving his family and I think he wanted to be something completely new. He had a very inventive brain. He was so clever that he could invent anything and you would just believe it. He was not the sort of man you would question.'

O'Brian was perhaps not as secretive about his marriage to Sarah Jones as Dean King suggests. It was common knowledge among his friends in the late 1950s, although it was a subject best avoided at Collioure.

'Mary O'Brian was his second wife and we all knew that,' says Mary. 'But we never talked about it.' She also knew that O'Brian had changed his name and that he had at one time worked as a taxi driver in London.

'Mary told me. He went round telling people it was an ambulance. In his later life he didn't want people to know that he drove a taxi.'

On several occasions Mary met Richard O'Brian, who has described his father as 'stern and intolerable'. Dean King says that their relationship never improved during Richard's summer sojourns at Collioure, although the boy became very fond of Mary O'Brian. O'Brian and son last met in 1963 and cut off contact with each other thereafter.

'Richard was coming out every summer. I think I was there when he first started. I met him and we got on very well. He was slightly unsure of himself. He wasn't very bouncy but he was very nice.' To her eyes O'Brian shared a good relationship with Richard and with his stepson Nikolai.

As to the truth about O'Brian's sailing prowess?

'I never saw him go sailing and he didn't have a boat when I was there. I have a funny feeling he didn't sail.'

In autumn 1963 Alice and Ridley, frail and sickly octogenarians, returned to England for the last time and settled in a residential home in Grasmere. They would both die within two years. In December 1963 Mary returned to France to collect the proceeds from the sale of their house, having decided to drive the profits out of the country in order to avoid bank charges. Accompanied by her friend Ellen Huddlestone Mary sailed to the Boulogne ferry terminal and drove south. On the Collioure coast she met her parents' adipose agent Vegand, who handed the proceeds in cash. It was too little but Mary did not feel confident enough to argue the technicalities.

'We agreed everything, had the sad task of collecting things from the house and arranging for the sale of the rest,' she wrote in her diary. 'It had been their little paradise in the sun for nearly fifteen years but this was a sad moment. Sadder still when I took Mummy's precious violin back in the boot and it cracked.'

Business over, Mary and Ellen headed north as winter weather raced after them, the roads glittering with ice, a blizzard breaking overhead. At a little town called Gasé the Mini shuddered to a halt in the snow.

'Some young boys helped to push us off the road to the hotel garage and we were at first the only guests. There were two worries plaguing me. First of all, our green card expired in two days and secondly, how was I going to smuggle the money out?'

By the following noon the snow had stopped falling and the sun had emerged. They continued the journey. After a fretful night in a Boulogne hotel, Mary, racked with worry about the money, stuffed it into a belt around her waist and drove onto the ferry. The crossing was rough and Mary, thousands of francs stitched around her, glowed green. She disappeared below decks. At English customs she was sure she would be unmasked as a smuggler. The Customs Officer took one look at her white face and knew just what was wrong. The best way to beat seasickness, he said, is to wear a tight belt around your tummy. Then he waved her through.

Ambleside

HOLIDAYS IN THE PYRENEES ELEVATED mountain walking into the pantheon of Mary's pastimes and she developed a passion for rugged landscapes. So in 1955, when a teacher-training college in the Lake District town of Ambleside advertised a vacancy for an art lecturer's post, Mary successfully applied. She would leave the flat Vale of Warwick for the Cumbrian fells.

Charlotte Mason established her House of Education for governesses in 1892, writing to friends that she felt the distance from London would work in her favour; students would be inspired by the beauty of peaks, passes, valleys, lakes and waterfalls. A Victorian pedagogical pioneer whose 1886 book *Home Education* ran to many editions and who was instrumental in the formation of the Parents National Education Union (PNEU), Mason was fifty when she founded the Lake District school with a roll-call of just four students. The principles of the PNEU and the House of Education challenged the Victorian view of how children should be educated. Instead of being 'seen but not heard', they were to be treated instead as individuals, each requiring stimulation from an early age by a broad curriculum – ideas that may be given today, but were revolutionary in Mason's time.

The House of Education became Charlotte Mason College following its founder's death and remained a teacher training school for women – kept under the broad umbrella of the PNEU. It is today a mixed-sex teacher-training outpost of St Martin's College, Lancaster with some 800 full-time undergraduate students, set among the spectacular fells above Windermere.

It was not long after she arrived at the college that Mary became 'fired up'. She built a kiln in the grounds and so sculpture and pottery were quickly added to the curriculum, Mary ably assisted by the Ambleside potter George Cook.

Jocelyn Davison, a former Charlotte Mason pupil who now lives the life of a sheep farmer's wife in New Zealand, remembers:

'She captured our immature imaginations and held them throughout her lessons. She had an incredibly broad knowledge and was always full of encouragement. In fact, I don't really even think of our times with her as "lessons" because they were such fun in the best sense. We loved learning from her and making things with her. We had great respect for her. She never "sucked up" to us or tried to be nice. It was the sheer force of her own enthusiasm for her subjects that carried us along and opened our eyes to the value of creativity and history.

'I have to say that these have remained lifelong passions of my own and I am sure many other of her pupils. Cicero opined that not to know history was to remain a child all your life. Mary helped us all grow up.'

The new teacher was also quick to embrace the social scene; Mary regularly broke the college nine o'clock curfew without detection, having persuaded students not to shut the fire escape. On one afternoon, keen to attend a soirée on Windermere's shore with her friend Libby Fothergill, but stranded due to lack of transport, she stepped into a local garage and bought an Austin Seven for £50 cash.

Mary was driving this little car, one hand gripping a gear stick which would otherwise slip into neutral, when she was flagged down by two excited students in 1958 and duly embroiled in an odd affair. The students had seen a figure tied up in the front passenger seat of a blue Austin Twelve further along the road. The unlucky passenger was writhing and kicking, trying to break free of his ropes. The students remained hidden behind a low wall, uncertain what to do. Before they could act, a second man, wearing a cap and an old coat, arrived, climbed in and drove off. Eventually a description was dispatched to the police. The budding Miss Marples of Charlotte Mason suspected kidnapping or worse but at supper that evening, as the gossip of the unfortunate man was passed around the table, one of the older students suddenly remembered seeing something very similar weeks before.

'It was a Sunday morning and I was walking in the lonely road between Windermere and Bowness when I saw a man tied up in the car,' she recalled. 'I thought it was rather queer and felt I must retrace a few steps and offer him some assistance; this I did and he said it was all right, his wife had done it for a joke. This seemed very strange and so I went on and thought I would call in at the police station. That was a mile off, and when I'd reached it my story seemed so weird that I thought it was better to forget the whole affair.' Days later the police confirmed that Ambleside was indeed plagued by a serial escapologist who got his kicks from being tied up in his own car (with the aid of his wife or a man in a dirty old coat). There was no law against this hobby, said the police, and it was difficult to know how to 'get him'.

Howard Somervell's adventures with ropes were more conventional. Mary met this doctor and famous mountain climber soon after she moved to Ambleside. Somervell had worked as a missionary medic in India and was a member of the 1922 and 1924 attempts on Everest. He climbed in tweeds and thick woollen jumpers in an age that venerated condensed milk and distrusted oxygen masks. When Mary first encountered Somervell he lived above Ambleside, in a spot now overlooking a nursery garden, and he was often seen climbing the fells or skating on Rydal lake in winter.

Both of Somervell's Everest attempts failed, ending in disaster and death. The 1922 expedition was led by 56-year-old General Charles Granville Bruce. On 7 June of that year, after the early arrival of the Himalayan monsoon, Somervell made a final attempt on Everest's peak as part of a team that included George Mallory, who was to die on the mountain two years later. The party was struck by an avalanche below the North Col of Everest. Seven porters were killed. Any further attempt that year was ruled out.

When Somervell returned in 1924 it was again as part of an expedition commanded by General Bruce. Two weeks after setting out from Darjeeling, Bruce fell ill with malaria and returned to base. Edward Norton took charge and, with George Mallory, decided to place three camps, at 7,750, 8,000 and 8,300 metres respectively, and to make two simultaneous attempts at the final ascent. Bad weather set in and two sherpas died of frostbite. When four other sherpas became stuck in a snowbound camp, Somervell was among the party that succeeded in rescuing them. On 2 June Somervell and Edward Norton started out from the 7,750 metre camp in a final push for the summit. Somervell began to have difficulty breathing and Norton suffered the first symptoms of snow-blindness; he had forgotten to bring his protective glasses. Eventually the pair were forced to descend and Somervell began coughing continuously. He thought he was dying. In despair, he hit himself on the chest and a gobbet of mucus shot up his throat. Blood rose to his mouth but he could breathe again. Both men reached the camp where Mallory and others were perched. During the night Norton experienced a blinding pain in his eyes. He was suffering from severe ophthalmia and would be completely blind for sixty hours.

On 6 June Mallory set off with the young climber Andrew Irvine for another dash at Everest glory. Two days later, as they left the highest camp for a place in the history books, the weather was fine. Team geologist Noel Odell watched them as they crossed a snowy ridge below the summit. Clouds soon swept over the mountain and it began to snow. Irvine and Mallory were never seen alive again. No one knew if they had reached the summit. The expedition was over.

The story was not. Mallory had carried a camera. Inside it may be the answer to the question that has puzzled mountaineers for decades – whether Mallory and Irvine conquered Everest twenty-nine years before the triumphant ascent of Edmund Hillary and Sherpa Tenzing Norgay. They would certainly have taken a picture of the summit if they had reached it. Kodak says the film the pair used might well have been preserved by the extreme cold and that, if the camera were found, it may be possible to develop it.

In May 1999 American climbers discovered Mallory's body and brittle clothes – but no camera. The hunt continues. One man with a particular interest in that search is Graham Hoyland.

'Mallory was carrying a Vest-Pocket Kodak camera lent to him by Howard Somervell, who had returned to the North Col after his own nearly successful attempt a few days before,' Hoyland told newspaper reporters. 'Somervell, my great-uncle, told me the Mallory story when I was 14.'

Photographs weren't the only visual records of that expedition. Somervell had taken rough brown paper and paints on his Everest attempts and produced many sketches and paintings. One of them, a picture of a blue lake gouged into the rock 16,000 feet up Everest, hangs in Mary's bedroom at Isel Hall in Cumbria.

'He thought he was probably the first westerner to have seen it because it was off the track,' she says. 'They were on their day off and they weren't climbing, they were resting. He went on his own for a walk and came across this brilliantly blue sapphire lake lost in the folds of the mountain.'

Somervell could be a brusque man – repeatedly rejecting Mary's encouragement that he sell his work or sharply refusing her offer of help when he struggled with his coat after a dark evening's ice-skating on Rydal – but they nevertheless became good friends. Mary persisted in her attempts to buy some of his work and one day Somervell suddenly changed his mind, casually offering to sell her some sketches and an oil. 'I need the money,' he explained. Mary wasn't the only buyer. Abbot Hall Gallery – Mary had become its Director by this time – acquired a Tibet mountain scene for one shilling. (Somervell insisted on the token because he did not want future directors to think the painting had been 'foisted' on the gallery, Mary explains.)

'He was very modest about painting. He was a brilliant doctor. He was very modest about everything he did.'

While wandering through Ambleside one summer's day in 1956 Mary met Zillah Brown and Thella Marriott, two local ladies busy with good works in the town and far beyond. They invited her to a United Nations meeting taking place that evening. It was an event that would change her life. Sat beside Frank Thompson, the headmaster of Ambleside Junior School, she watched a film about refugees living in camps in Austria. Eleven years after the end of the Second World War and the creation of the Iron Curtain, central Europe was still home to thousands of refugees, stranded by war or fleeing communism, yet to be repatriated or found a foster state. The film showed people living in the bare huts of former concentration camps, emaciated and desperate. As the reel told its sorry tale, several people in the audience began to cry – including Frank Thompson and Mary. When the house lights flickered into life overhead and a UN spokesman asked for volunteers to travel to Austria to build houses for the refugees, Frank and Mary raised their hands.

They travelled in trucks across Europe, two Charlotte Mason students in tow, and set to work in camps around Linz, Austria, building houses for refugees from Eastern Europe who had fought alongside the Nazis – Romanians, Hungarians, Latvians, Poles and Lithuanians – all hungry and homeless, many suffering mental trauma.

Much of the volunteers' work involved making bricks for these new buildings. There were other, less savoury jobs. In the Wegsheid camp, sixty families were given two toilets and when one of them became blocked, a dearth of suitable tools meant Mary had to clear it with her bare hands. In another camp the volunteers spent a day clearing rotting clothing and excrement from the basement of their hut. Over the next three summers the Ambleside volunteers took sixty people, many Charlotte Mason College students, to help at the camps for three or four weeks. For some, the experience was too potent – Mary remembers one student who broke down sobbing after visiting Mauthausen, a former concentration camp.

On one occasion Mary found herself sitting on a sickbed beside Sue Ryder, a remarkable woman who had served with the Polish Section of the highly secret Special Operations Executive during the war, and whose relief work inspired her to create the Sue Ryder Foundation, which provides over eighty homes in twenty countries for disabled and sick people of all ages. Sue Ryder in turn introduced Mary to Joyce Pearce, co-founder of the Ockenden Venture, a charity that provided homes for refugee children in Britain. The meeting inspired Mary and the other eleven Ambleside volunteers to consider fundraising for an Ockenden house in their home town. They created a committee and, despite some local opposition, collecting groups blossomed in Ambleside, Ulverston and Keswick. Mary embarked on a fifty-date lecture tour on the plight of the refugees, curing herself of an earlier aversion to public speaking as she travelled from school hall to village church.

The first Ockenden children arrived in 1961, a ragged bunch of Polish and Yugoslavian girls with not one word of English between them, bound for Millans Park in Ambleside under the care of 'housemother' Dorothy Taylor. They included one girl – little Antonina – whose buttoned-up boots hid severely deformed feet and who would be swiftly despatched to the Ethel Hedley hospital at Calgarth Park and the care of local orthopaedic surgeon Mr Cuppage. Another girl, having been separated from two younger siblings bound for Italy, tried to throw herself out of an upstairs window. For most children, however, the experience was a happy one. The Ockenden Venture homes gave them an education and stable home environment for two or three years and returned them to their families with hopefully a brighter future ahead of them. The Ockenden home in Ambleside closed only a few years ago, ending its days as a haven for Tibetan refugees fleeing Chinese rule.

CHAPTER 4

Persia

WHEN THE YOUNG PERSIAN Shi'ite Muslim Hasan-i-Sabbah joined the heretical Isma'ilian sect in 1071 he launched one of the most effective terrorist groups in history. From the Isma'ilians he gathered warriors, pronouncing himself their Grand Master and exhorting them to murder his enemies, slitting throats and sprinkling poisons on dark nights. Lurid stories of Hasan's ruthlessness were spread by Crusaders returning to Europe; in secret gardens Hasan fed his recruits hashish to secure their loyalty and dull their consciences. Thus they became 'hashishiyyin' – the Assassins.

The Assassins' power in Persia, though tremendous, was short-lived. When the Mongol armies under Hulagu Khan swept east in 1256 across the Elburz Mountains they took one Assassin fortress after the other, carrying out their sieges with scientific precision under the guidance of Chinese engineers.

'Hulagu . . . took and destroyed among others fifty or more castles of the Assassins. Of all these strongholds, which one hears of over the north of Persia [modern day Iran] from the borders of Khoresan to those of Iranian Iraq, only two are mentioned as having put up any long resistance. These are Girdkuh and Lamiasar, of which the sites have hitherto been unknown. They held out for six months . . . and the story goes that, as far as Girdkuh is concerned, it could have resisted even longer, but was forced to capitulate owing to a shortage not of food and water, but of clothes.'

So wrote Dame Freya Stark, adventurer, writer, archaeologist, geographer, diplomat, journalist and Orientalist. Stark began her travels in the Middle East while on Government service in the 1930s, exploring Persia, Turkey, Arabia and Afghanistan, crossing areas no European women and few European men had ever seen. Travel, she said, was in her blood. (At the age of four she had boarded a ship on her own, carrying only a mackintosh under her arm, a toothbrush and one halfpenny.)

During the Second World War Stark helped persuade the Arabs to remain neutral towards the British Empire when Rommel tried to wrestle away the Empire's hold on the Middle East. After 1945 she devoted herself to writing and retracing Alexander's march of conquest through the western half of the Persian Empire of his time, which extended into modern day Turkey; she learnt the language by picking through Turkish translations of English detective stories she knew, improving her pronunciation by listening to restaurant waiters and store clerks in Istanbul. She wrote more than twenty books about her adventures; the apogee of her career was probably *Rome on the Euphrates*, an investigation of the Roman Empire's exploration of the Middle East, which took her three years to write and was published in 1966, when she was 73. Six years later she was made a Dame of the British Empire.

Stark's research into the Assassins' castles was an earlier triumph. By 1931 she had completed three dangerous treks into the wilderness of western Iran, hunting for ruins among the Elburz Mountains. The book she wrote about her adventures – *The Valleys of the Assassins* – received immediate acclaim upon its publication in 1934. It is a travel and adventure classic, at times hauntingly beautiful. It describes Stark's travels into Luristan, the mountainous region between Iraq and present-day Iran, and her intrepid journey to Lamiasar, the castle famed for its defence by the Assassins against invading Mongol tribes. She did not find, however, the castle at Girdkuh.

So Mary Burkett set out to find it in her stead. She sought also the castle-cracking Hulagu, supposedly entombed in the mystical island of Shahi, and, eventually, Dame Freya herself. It was an adventure of a lifetime. It would lead Mary to wild wolves, religious fanatics, desert storms, gunfire in the dark and the most beautiful city in the world.

Mary's adventure began as she walked over Kendal's Whitbarrow Fell with Genette Malet de Carteret, a young lawyer who had volunteered to teach English in the Ockenden home at Ambleside. Daughter of a prominent Jersey family whose ancestral fires flickered in the Norman manor at St Ouen's, Genette had just finished reading law at Lady Margaret Hall in Oxford. As she paced the hills she pondered a career as a barrister and made mental notes about her four suitors – the German, the Greek, the French and the English man.

To Mary and the other Ockenden volunteers Genette was invaluable, bright and friendly, a good English teacher who tackled the more menial jobs in the Ockenden home with verve. Mary had introduced Genette to friends, taken her to parties and tried to keep her entertained. Here, standing among the mountains, the conversation turned to adventure and the pair discovered, quite by accident, that they both harboured an ambition to travel to Persia. After a brief discussion they impetuously declared a pact: they would leave their jobs and set off on an eastern adventure.

The trip took a year to plan. Genette enrolled on a Land-Rover driving and mechanics course and both women began to read frantically about Persia, Freya Stark's books high on the reading list. They resolved to make the search for Girdkuh castle an integral part of their adventure. The tomb of the Mongol Hulagu, supposedly encased in the great Dadan Rock on the island of Shahi west of the town of Tabriz, was their second goal. They also contacted the Institute of Persian Studies in Tehran, and David Stronach, an archaeologist with the Institute, invited them to spend ten weeks of their trip helping out at the dig he was running on the Turcoman Steppe in northern Persia.

The women organised sponsorship and began to pack the Land-Rover with Complan packs, canned fruit, steak and kidney puddings and blancmange. They hung a net under the roof, to hammock supplies that would be moved to create space for sleeping bodies; they would spend most nights in the vehicle, a cosh and a carton of pepper carried for defence, forgetting either was there until the carton of black grains broke open one day in the hot desert, and loud reports of sneezing ricocheted around the vehicle.

As the departure date of 18 March 1962 grew closer, Mary resigned from her post at Charlotte Mason College. She would not have to worry about finding a new job on her return; Francis Scott, Chairman of the Abbot Hall Art Gallery in Kendal and (along with his wife Frieda) a good friend of Mary's, offered her a place as assistant to the gallery's director Helen Kapp on her return.

By March they were ready. At Ambleside, colleagues and students gave them a stirring send-off and at Kendal friends offered eggs and bread, cheering as they rolled along the first yards of an Arabian adventure that would take them thousands of miles, into desert and jungle, mud huts and magnificent mosques – that is until, just outside Kendal, the Land-Rover broke down. Mary and Genette, feeling a little silly, had to walk to the nearest garage and ask for assistance. The mechanic, looking over the engine, discovered that an important screw was missing. He quickly replaced it, watched eagerly by both women, who had seen enough to perform the same procedure when it fell out again 500 miles later.

The journey proper began. From Dover they sailed to Calais and drove through France, Italy and on to Yugoslavia, ducking behind the Iron Curtain. They raced through the night between high walls of snow that threatened to collapse over the vehicle. In Bulgaria they stopped in a small town to be served thin soup and warm fists of black bread. They were in a hurry – their visas would last for only a few more hours and they had to reach the border before nightfall – but two burly medical students invited them to share a drink in their flat, where they begged to be smuggled into Turkey. Mary and Genette refused. At the border the police searched the Land-Rover from bumper to bumper.

After a night asleep in the van they stood stiff and cold before an old Turkish mosque and ate a breakfast of omelette sprinkled with orange slices, paid for by a stranger who simply muttered 'Chok guzel' (very beautiful) and shuffled away along the road. Via Istanbul and Ankara they drove on to Tehran, where they met David Stronach, the man in charge of the dig at Gunbad-i-Qabus to the north-east. The journey had taken them two weeks. The dig was delayed, snagged on Persian red tape, so the women decided to set off in search of the lost Assassins' castle and join David later.

They drove east, practising their Farsi and suffering the curious courtesy of the Savak, the Shah's secret police, whose agents would occasionally usher them into humid offices and examine their papers. Though infamously cruel to their countrymen, the Savak were reliably genteel with Genette and Mary; breaking away from an indifferent interrogation, they would suddenly start talking about the weather or offer to buy the women bread. A greater threat lay on the roadside. The long-distance truck drivers had a bad reputation, so every evening the women drove off the road, away from the sweep of a lorry's lights. If they stopped in a town they slept in small teahouses or, if the town was large enough, a hotel.

At Damghan they searched for a place to sleep outside the city walls, eventually parking the Land-Rover on a dry riverbed. In the middle of the night lightning began to flicker across the sky, accompanied by the drumming of thunder. Although rain danced on the roof, it soon subsided, as did the women's worries that they might be swept away by water rushing down the wadi. In the morning, under a clear blue sky, they began looking for the castle of Girdkuh and met an old man throwing gravel into potholes along the road.

'Girdkuh?' they enquired, without much expectation of a reply.

'*Ham unja!* [Over there!]' he said, pointing over the flat plain towards the mountains. Mary and Genette were amazed but, sure enough, they could just make out the hunched shoulders of a castle, perched high on a round mountain seven miles away.

The women drove away from the main road, through a maze of boulders and across a gravel plain, their eyes fixed on the distant castle, the desert a dusty dilapidated beige as the day waned. When they reached the foot of the mountain, they walked on until they spotted a track shooting up to the summit, the first twenty feet of which had been washed away. After another restless night in the Land-Rover, Mary crossing her legs as jackals stalked outside and screamed at the moon, the women peered out from behind the curtains to find a tall, solemn young man leaning on his shepherd's crook and staring incredulously back at them. 'He had never seen Western women before,' wrote Mary. 'He'd never even been to Tehran. So we got out carefully and offered him some Kendal mint cake. We said it was English sugar. He must have thought he was seeing things.'

Mary and Genette began to climb, the shepherd's flute conjuring a tune from below. Above them stood the castle 'so steep, when one looks up one's cap falls off' (as Marco Polo wrote) and defended so valiantly by its Assassin keepers, who flung stone balls from the ramparts to repel the Mongol invaders. When the women finally reached the castle, the desert sun beating down, they found it was littered with these 'cannon balls'. They also found a pigeon tower, coins, gold, a fossilised beehive, and shards of crockery – all dating back to the ninth century.

'Pottery of all shapes and sizes was strewn about,' wrote Mary. 'There were the remains of a possible kiln, where large pieces of fired drainpipe and tile still lay together. The great front wall, with its elaborate trefoil windows, clung precariously to the rock as if conscious of an impending crash. It was crumbling far too danger-ously for our close approach. We were fascinated by three huge water-storing tanks, their plaster linings still intact – one the size of a small swimming pool and the others smaller.'

The scorching sun forced them to begin the descent. The cannon ball they chose as a souvenir for Dr Laurence Lockhart, a scholar who knew of Girdkuh, was too awkward to carry, so they rolled it down the mountain. Genette was feeling weak, struck by a stomach bug, and they rested every few minutes.

'Once nearly down we made our way in the evening heat towards the van, but before we had emerged from the rough valley Genette's remaining strength had left her, and she was forced to lie down in a small hewn cave, probably the shelter of some shepherd.'

Mary picked her way to the van, worrying that wolves might be prowling near Genette's cave. After half an hour she reached the Land-Rover, and drove slowly over very rocky ground nearer the mountain and closer to the ailing Genette, who staggered towards the vehicle.

By the 1960s the tall Turcoman nomads who had historically ranged over the Russian steppe with their flocks, occasionally making raids on to the high Iranian plateau, had been hemmed into a narrow corridor of land by the Persian government. Gunbad-i-Qabus is an agricultural trade town on this Turcoman Steppe, sitting under the shadow of the eastern Elburz Mountains. The town takes its name from the brick burial tower which shoots 168 feet up from the plain, pencil point piercing the dusty desert haze, exquisite Kufic script curled around its walls. The Gunbad was built as the tomb of Qabus ibn Washmgir – an astrologer, poet, calligrapher and patron of the arts who reigned in the province until his 1012 assassination. According to legend, Qabus's body was suspended in a glass coffin within an inner dome so that the sun, striking through an eastern opening, would meet him every morning.

It was to Gunbad that Mary and Genette drove on their return from Girdkuh, to be met by a policeman in the smart blue and gold uniform of the Shahrbani. He in turn escorted them to the house of one Kamyab, the town's vice-head of education, for whom they possessed a letter of introduction. Here they found a small door in a long wall, the perfume of orange blossom drifting through the garden, the walls of the house beyond covered in the magnificent deep red and black of Turcoman carpets. Saddlebags were draped over the chairs, and a pyramid of little cushions, with wonderfully fine weave, stood precariously on the chaise-longue.

Kamyab appeared. He was short, fat, well-dressed and spoke schoolboy French. After a brief conversation punctuated by pauses as Kamyab felt for a word, the women explained that they must leave for the police station, where they were to have their Savak cards checked and then sleep the night, a proposal that delighted their policeman guide. Despite the faltering exchange it wasn't the last they were to see of Mr Kamyab. They were to spend much of their time in Gunbad sipping glasses of sweet tea or wandering around the town's carpet shops with the charming little man. Later he was to accompany them on a dangerous pilgrimage.

First there was yet another delay at the dig so Mary and Genette decided to bide their time exploring the Russian frontier and the remains of Qizil Alan, or Alexander's Wall (which was actually built by the Persian Sassanian dynasty in the sixth century). They passed small villages of Turcoman huts with felt roofs and, after a worrying night when a lorry driver tapped on their windows then retreated into the dark, reached the little town of Gumshan, a few miles from the shore of the Caspian.

'Dried fish were hanging from the houses, and Turcoman rugs peculiar to this area, with strange primitive designs and whorls and curves, were spread over the wooden balconies. The women here for the first time were keen to be photographed and clustered round us, laughing at these visitors from another world,' wrote Genette.

'We went on over the mudflats, absorbed by the black-headed wagtails hopping about in the scanty grass. The shore stretched muddily for miles in both directions and we shaded our eyes towards the Russian frontier. Two or three rough flat-bottomed wooden boats were drawn up, and just as we were finding paddling impracticable in the knee-deep mud, a friendly fisherman came up.'

He offered them a ride in his boat, and with a few deft movements of his punting pole they slid over the mud onto the water. Fish were jumping everywhere. It was nine o'clock in the morning. Back on shore, they found a policeman pacing up and down beside the Land-Rover.

'He was incensed with us because Gumshan was not mentioned on our Savak travel cards and with the [Turcoman] fisherman for taking us out in the boat at all, though at the time we could not understand why. Gestures of throat-slitting and stealing were intended to indicate that Turcomans were a shifty and unreliable lot, a fact which the gently troubled face of the fisherman completely belied.'

They were escorted to the local police station, given fizzy drinks and dried fish, driven on to the station at Bandar Shah, offered tea and cakes then invited to leave after a cursory inspection of their passports. Thus the Savak attempted to discourage foreigners from approaching the Russian frontier.

Back in Gunbad they were assigned a room in the archaeological team's house. They waited for the rest of the group to arrive, spending long, hot, idle days sitting cross-legged on their veranda as they watched a Persian general totter past in his pyjamas – until the sultry morning that Mary made a discovery which would have a profound effect upon her life. In a nearby street a woman and a child were rolling a bundle of fabric over a bed of leaves. Mary was fascinated. She watched as the couple snatched and tugged at the wide woollen square, rolling it into a tight cylinder. Mother and daughter were making a felt rug.

As Mary explains in the book she would later write on the subject, feltmaking is an ancient art. Evidence of felt goods has emerged from archaeological sites like Çatal Hüyük in Turkey, which revealed a 6,500 BC city rich in the feltmaker's art. Fine felt rugs were found in Pazyryk mounds in the Altai mountains of Siberia, where archaeological evidence dated felt activity from the seventh to second century BC. In Homer's Iliad felt caps are common and Odysseus was said to have worn a helmet lined with felt. Herodotus remarks on the Persian habit of wearing felt skull-caps, and at the funeral of Alexander in 324 BC the pyre was draped with a piece of scarlet felt. From the Greeks felt passed to the Romans. A coin commemorating the assassination of Julius Caesar in 44 BC shows a felt cap flanked by two daggers. Suetonius, in his *Life of Nero*, describes Rome's citizens as 'the felted mob'. Genghis Khan's collective designation for the unified Turko-Mongolian tribes of Asia was 'the generations that live in felt tents'. There is a tradition of feltmaking across Europe, Asia, Africa and the Middle East.

Felt is most often created from wool – other materials are employed to produce patterns in a rug or cape. Fine hairs, like those of the camel, are used for making felt caps. Felt is not woven; the process depends upon the fibre's propensity for naturally binding together if pressure, heat and moisture are applied. To make a felt rug, for instance, wool is teased and combed. The wool is beaten out and laid over reed mats, sacking or a bed of leaves. Usually soap is sprinkled or spread onto the matting first, and if the felt is to be patterned, the coloured wool for the pattern is often laid on the matting first. The wool is arranged differently according to whether it will become a coat, a tent roof or a rug. Hot water is then sprinkled over it and the whole felt is then rolled up tightly and tied evenly. Knees, elbows, forearms or feet are used to supply adequate force for up to an hour. The roll is then untied, unevenness is padded out, edges are straightened and more hot water and soap are applied. The rolling begins again and continues for three or four hours.

The felt is then 'fulled' to make it smoother. In Turkey this was traditionally done in steamy baths, where the material was rolled back and forth on the marble floors. Soap and water are used once more and the workers don't stop until the fibres are properly matted together. Sometimes resin is added to give extra strength. Finally the felt is rubbed smooth by hand and any soap washed out.

This process, first witnessed in that small desert town, so intrigued Mary that she determined to learn more about felt and feltmaking. She would become one of the world's most eminent experts on felt. In 1979 she would write *The Art of the Felt Maker*, probably the seminal work on the subject, organising an exhibition of the same name at Abbot Hall Gallery in Kendal to mark the book's publication. She is the President of the International Felt Association, has lectured on felt across Europe and continues to be fascinated by this often-neglected art. To mark the Millennium, a Dutch felt-fanatical friend of Mary's called Inge Evers asked feltmakers from around the world to create felt flowers for a special 'mille fleurs' carpet. This was Mary's reward for her contribution to the understanding of felt. For four days in May members of the association gathered in Kendal to knead, tweak and full flowers into this magic carpet. On the Saturday they presented their gift to Mary at Charlotte Mason College.

'They came in pairs bearing the carpet on their heads, and passing it forward they crouched down and spread it before my feet,' says Mary. 'It was a very dramatic and emotional moment, and very hard to keep a steady voice when thanking them . . . I'll never forget it.' The floral wonder is now spread over a special room at Isel Hall.

Finally the dig began at Yarim Tepé, a few miles outside Gunbad. Mary was assigned the task of photographing and drawing pots. The

Tepé, or archaeological mound, had been sawn in half by the force of a river, its Persian treasures exposed. Progress was slowed by some of the workers hired from Gunbad.

'There were people taking hashish and they were very pathetic,' remembers Mary. Her own work was hampered by an infection in both her eyes that made it hard for her to see. There was no eye lotion or bath in the medical kit, so Mr Kamyab offered to take her to the doctor, a tall Persian called Abdul Khadjeh who spoke perfect English. Khadjeh's wife was a Welsh nurse called Gwen whom he had met while studying medicine in Wrexham. After treating Mary, Dr Khadjeh insisted that she and Genette come round and meet Gwen that evening.

This was the first of many visits they were to make to his home, for Gwen was longing for English company. When she heard that the women had nothing but a pump to wash under, she invited them to take a shower every day in the flat. There were other guests besides Genette and Mary however – the house was a refuge for opium addicts. Dr Khadjeh had begun prescribing a new drug course for patients and felt that addicts would be better off treated close-by rather than at home, where they might have access to opium. It was a traumatic time for Gwen. The patients would wander about the flat at night, screaming for release from fever and cramp as the drug drained from their bodies.

'They were dirty, unshaven, had never slept in a bed or used a shower before,' wrote Genette. 'Gwen gave them all their meals which, in their apathetic state, they merely picked at, and administered the necessary injections every few hours, where her nursing experience came in useful. The men were not locked in or restrained in any way. If they rampaged too much at night, Abdul stormed in and told them to leave if they could not keep quiet, which would sober them because the cure, though immediately expensive, would mean endless savings in the future.

'After some days they returned home and the news soon got about that the cure had been successful. From then on a steady stream of men came to spend a couple of weeks there, sometimes shuffling past as we sat talking on the veranda, or leaning over the baby's pram to rock it a little.'

One day Gwen, Genette and Mary decided to drive out into the jungle for a picnic, huddling into the doctor's car with the baby and the maid. When they found a pretty spot they stopped, laid out a magnificent Turcoman rug, filled the samovar and devoured the food. Driving home in the dark Mary hit a pile of earth and then, as she pushed her foot down hard on the brakes, a second and a third. The front axle snapped and the engine juddered to a halt. No one was hurt but the jungle began to rumble with nocturnal noises. The hours passed slowly by until a truck's lights winked in the distance. The vehicle came to a halt beside the car and a group of men jumped out, each carrying a machine gun. They offered to take the stranded picnickers back to Gunbad. The women had no choice but to accept, leaving the luggage behind, a gun barrel bouncing beside Mary's knee, the gun's safety catch flipped to 'off'. The men's word was good and they drove the party to the house of the doctor, who was away visiting a patient in a distant village. Genette and Mary stole upstairs and climbed into their sleeping bags, exhausted.

'I remember about three o'clock in the morning and Abdul tiptoed in saying, "I'm sorry my car let you down." "I am so sorry," I said. "It wasn't your car, it was me." He wouldn't take a penny, anything.' By the time they emerged for breakfast the vehicle had been repaired.

The city of Meshed on the far north-eastern corner of Persia houses the gold-domed shrine of the eighth Imam Ali Reza, and is the most holy site in Iran for Shi'ite pilgrims. It is also an important centre for carpet manufacturing and turquoise, lifted from the mines at nearby Nishapur. When the dig halted for two days in the Muslim holiday of Moharram, Genette and Mary decided to seize the opportunity to travel east to Meshed – even though it was considered unsafe for Europeans to be seen on the streets during this time of often-fanatical worship. Mr Kamyab asked if he could accompany them. He had been such a good friend they couldn't refuse him.

Approaching the city they stopped for the night in a small village and were just falling asleep in a room overlooking the main street when they were jerked alert by the boom of an approaching drum – deep, rhythmic and menacing. Peering gingerly out of the window they saw the street thronged with black-shirted men. Every hundred yards or so the crowd stopped and a group of figures, either naked to the waist or wearing strange cut-away black vests, started a throbbing urgent song and dance. The men beat their chests and whipped themselves with metal chains, their backs and shoulders soon glistening with blood.

'Ya Ali, Ya Hossein,' they cried, evoking the names of their two most revered clerics.

Mr Kamyab – a Sunni – cowered behind the curtains in the next room, picturing the Shi'ite mob, dripping with blood, storming the hotel and flaying him to shreds. The songs and the wailings continued throughout the night, their strange vibrations eventually lulling the women to sleep. Kamyab, however, had no rest and when the group arrived in Meshed the next morning he suddenly announced that he was frightened of being seen with the two Europeans. He would not associate with them while they stayed in Meshed, he stuttered in his rickety French, and as they parked the car in the gardens of the British Consulate he disappeared in search of a hotel.

Kamyab had a point. Mary and Genette, in their western clothes, were shot long and disapproving glances by several men as they walked through the town that day. They decided to disguise themselves in chadors, the long cloths that enveloped the Meshed women from head to foot. Unfortunately, the chadors they were given by Persian friends in preparation for the Meshed trip were not as inconspicuous as they would have liked, one coloured blue and the other white with pink spots. However, each gave them enough cover to scuttle through the narrow streets in safety, avoiding the main procession of pilgrims. They followed a rabbit warren of streets from the bazaar to the gold minaret of Ali's shrine but on each approach were turned back by policemen, friendly but obstinate.

'They cannot risk any form of a riot, with the people in such a frenzied state,' wrote Genette. 'At the main square before the big gleaming mosaic clock tower, we were even turned back by officious little eight-year-old boys.' The women gave up trying to reach the shrine and set off to bargain for turquoises instead.

'That night the clear air was still full of the mourning chant of the mullahs, relayed by loudspeakers all over the city. The high-pitched nasal tones penetrated deep into our minds and became our most lasting impression of Meshed.'

Before they left they picked up an agitated Mr Kamyab. His worries blossomed further when the Land-Rover broke down. 'Ce n'est pas sauf pour moi,' he said again and again, rubbing his chubby hands. 'Ce n'est pas sauf pour moi either,' thought Mary as she stood stranded beside the car. 'Then a van came along and a big fat man and smaller man came out and said, "What's your problem?" So he opened the bonnet, twiddled a bit of wire and said, "Me Mechanica", beating his chest.'

The car started immediately. The party jumped in and thanked their rescuers, who would not take a penny in payment. Back at the dig the workers greeted Genette and Mary enthusiastically.

'Now you can call yourselves Meshedi,' they said. 'You have made the pilgrimage.'

Among the experts on the Gunbad team was orientalist David Bivar – now Professor Emeritus of Iranian Studies at London University. When the dig drew to a close, he joined Mary and Genette on a journey into the Elburz Mountains. They travelled first to Gurgan, a small town on the Caspian Sea, then to the mining settlement of Zirab and the beautiful tomb towers at Ladjim and Resget. At Pol-e-Sefid, the eponymous white bridge spanning the river Ahwaz, a charming young teacher called Ali Shokri dragged the local newspapermen up to the English party's campsite. They were followed by a deputation of town dignitaries: the postmaster, the army commandant, the stationmaster.

From Pol-e-Sefid the trio began their trek through the mountains, accompanied by muleteers who would burst into spontaneous song, their mutinous arguments with David broken by a bribe of blackberries. One night was spent in the house of the *khadkhoda*, or headman, of a village called Sangi-deh. His tiny home crouched beneath flat eaves and wooden shutters hung beside the holes that served for windows. An oil lamp shed a little light. The travellers were served great plates of eggs and rice and given glass after glass of tea. The next day they rode through high mountain passes and along tracks lined with wild strawberries, stopping at midday to take a picnic beside a stream chuckling with icy clear water. On their way down into the valleys they found another tomb tower, hidden among trees close to the path, smaller and less ornate than those at Resget and Ladjim, but still an interesting discovery to end the journey.

Glorious Isfahan beckoned. The women set out to the city through the dusty desert. The approach was depressing, wrote Genette:

'It was one of those sad stretches of country – sad from the point of view of its extreme aridity and infertility – grey colourless grit stretched to bleak eroded rocks whose formation looks as though it was the result of some violent upheavals . . . Excitement at last, there in the distance was a tiny blue speck in the centre of mud-coloured buildings – Isfahan!'

They drove through broad streets lined with trees, sweeping into the city whose name means 'half the world' – legend boasts that half the world is represented in its stunning architecture – and asking directions for the Mission Hospital where they had arranged to meet a Dr Wild. A small boy riding a bike beckoned them follow. The Land-Rover wound down a labyrinth of tiny alleys until at last they arrived at the main entrance to the hospital, from where they were directed to a nearby primary school, run by the Church of England diocese of Iran. Soon they were spreading baggage and mattresses across the schoolroom floor.

When the afternoon heat wore off, Mary and Genette ventured outside. Rounding the corner of the huge Maidan square, the women were spellbound by the surrounding wealth and colour. This was the splendour of Shah Abbas, the great king who made Isfahan his capital in the sixteenth century and who built the famous blue mosque over which the women marvelled as they walked within courtyards of glistening tiles.

'The sun shone on the great pale blue dome laced, as it were, with gorgeous patterns; its minarets soared upwards, their tiny gold tops dazzling in the light. All round the central courtyard were alcoves, arched and borne on pillars, again covered with this fantasy of design and intricacy of pattern. As the Muslim religion allows no human representation on religious buildings, all the designs must be floral, abstract or geometric, hence the almost bewildering mass of line and shape, yet at a distance each design glows with a light of its own.'

At Sheikh Lutfullah, a smaller mosque built by the Shah for his family, they admired the pale dome and the door decorated with a fine stalactite pattern. The prayer room bathed in a lime green light, it was a magical and sombre place. Opposite sat the Ali Qapu, the king's palace, from whose terraces Abbas watched polo games played out on the lawn below.

'The chief attraction of the Ali Qapu is now perhaps its finely decorated walls and ceilings,' wrote Genette. 'Many tiny little rooms have the most beautiful ceilings with fretted shapes of bottles and vases in wood and plaster. Here and there the remains of the blue and gold frescoes cling to the walls.'

Leaving the palace they stole through narrow alleyways, past vendors screaming out their wares, the air suffused with the smell of spices, animal skins and linseed oil. They passed old men smoking hashish pipes and metal smiths clinking and hammering their evening away. Children tugged at them and begged for money.

There were more mosques to see. Driving through the streets on their way to the mud-walled Jomeh Mosque, their taxi driver accidentally caught a woman's chador on his bumper, ripping it away from her.

'He laughed, but she was livid with rage at being thus exposed to full view, grabbed at it and made for him with her fists. They slapped each other for several seconds, she crying with rage, until another woman came to help her. She started biting the driver's hand till his smile changed to a wince, and he thought better of the affair and drove on.'

The next evening they crossed the famous Khadju bridge, another marvel built by order of Abbas (who would inspect his countrymen's craftsmanship in various disguises during different stages of construction). This was a bridge of banquet rooms, marriage feasts and holiday parties, designed so that at every point revellers could hear the sound of running water, little channels cut into the stone to amplify the sound of the river below. At night it swarmed with people . . .

'. . . like ants over the bridge; cyclists rode over it and barrow-boys sold their hot chestnuts, hot potatoes, sweet corn and drinks of all shades from yellow to magenta. Sounds of music, radios, instruments and singing filled the air. At the entrance a small beggar boy with a stump of a leg and completely blind dragged himself along by his hands. As we pushed some money into his little dusty fist, his eyeless expression changed and he muttered a long sentence of thanks. We felt very moved and tried in vain to find out his name.'

Eventually the two women resolved to set off into the desert, to make their way towards their second great goal of this adventure – the island of Shahi and Hulagu's tomb. They were sad to leave Isfahan, half the world. In the barren desert again, they watched a great spiral of dust spring up from the dry ground, like a listing tomb tower of sand, growing higher and higher till its top was lost in the clear azure sky.

At the dig they had promised to visit two boys called Keramat and Nasser when they came through to Pasargadae, then the British

Institute's main digging site and home to the tomb of Cyrus the Great, first Emperor of Persia, founder of the Achaemenid dynasty and the creator of the Cyrus Cylinder, considered to be the first declaration of human rights. It was at Pasargadae, which means Camp of the Persians, that Cyrus defeated his father-in-law, King of the Medes Astyages, in 550 BC and became the ruler of an immense empire which stretched from the Mediterranean to the Hindu Kush. The inscription on his small pointed stone tomb would have made Ozymandias blush. It read:

'O man whosoever thou are and whensoever comest (for that thou wilt come I know) I am Cyrus who founded the empire of the Persians. Grudge me not this little earth which covers my body.'

By the time Alexander the Great had defeated Darius III, the last of the Achaemenian emperors, and made himself the heir to the greatest empire the world had yet seen, the tomb had been defaced. Alexander, according to Arrian, was so upset to find the despoiled monument that the Magi who had been set to guard it were tortured on his command. (Plutarch says that he also slew the man responsible for the vandalism.)

Mary and Genette met Keramat at Pasargadae. Nasser was ill in hospital in Shiraz. Keramat, a bronze 16-year-old waiting for the next dig and a chance to work, took them to his family home in a nearby mud village.

'He led us up a few steps and into a tiny room, where we met his mother, a little middle-aged woman enveloped in different layers of clothing, with a kind, reliable face,' wrote Genette. 'There was a row of little brothers and sisters, none of whom had that pinched hard expression we had seen so often in these poor villages where children lived from hand to mouth, although their condition was no different from anyone else's.

'There were felt mats on the floor, and a couple of cushions. Keramat showed with immense pride the new oil lamp he had bought with his savings from the dig, and one or two treasured bowls and plates. This family was too poor even to afford a samovar, usually the staple possession of a Persian, and when Keramat offered us tea his mother disappeared outside to make a fire with dung on the threshold. The room was a mass or flies, swarming all over the sugar, and on the faces of the children.'

Mary and Genette were again touched by Persian hospitality but weighed-down by the poverty they saw. There was no work in

Pasargadae, unsanitary livestock shared the spring in Keramat's village, and the streets were piled with refuse and tumbledown walls. They refused lunch, knowing it would be beyond the household's meagre resources, and made their way to the city of Shiraz, pondering the iniquities of life.

After settling in Shiraz, they toured the estate of a kindly local landlord called Iradj. A handsome, well-built man who had studied law for a year at the Sorbonne, he made great efforts on behalf of the villagers working for him, supplying fresh water, decent housing and free medical care. He had a peculiarly gentle and restrained tone of voice when addressing them – firm yet unfailingly polite – and he was the antonym of the landlord they met a few days later in a hotel in Persepolis, an hour and a half's drive from Shiraz. This one invited them to spend the night on his estate.

'It appeared that he was an ardent admirer of Russia, a revolutionary, a tribal chieftain trying to establish the independence of his tribe, and yet also an extremely rich landowner,' wrote Genette. 'Half of his attitudes were incompatible, but he expounded them with such zest and enthusiasm that we forgave him his inconsistencies and listened fascinated.

'We swung off in his Russian Volga car which, though it looked like an ordinary saloon, could – as we saw later – give the performance of a Land-Rover. His house was very large, and far more palatial than any we had seen outside Tehran; in particular the bathroom and lavatory were completely clean and modern. Late into the night he told us more about his early life – how his father had died when he was young, and that he had had to shoot his way to manhood and leadership of his tribe; of the many enemies he had, and how he had been shot up not so long ago in Shiraz – he had an aura of Balkan revolution about him.'

He kept a gun in his pocket at all times and the mirror in his living room reflected both entrances, so he could see if anyone was approaching.

Returning to Shiraz, Mary and Genette told their hostess about this encounter and she burst out laughing. Their revolutionary was a notorious figure.

'He had a wife who was as much a tribal firebrand as himself, and she now lived separated from him in a house in Shiraz. But her jealousy and possessiveness were still unbounded. The story went that she had heard on one occasion that a woman had spent the night with her husband on his estate. Some days later she had lured the wretched woman into a lonely field and shot her dead. No one had dared to bring the force of the law upon her even if anything could be proved. Perhaps we had had a lucky escape, we thought. It would be best to leave Shiraz hastily.'

Mary and Genette crossed the desert to Ahwaz. Hot air rose from the burnt ground like flickering flame. It was 120 degrees Fahrenheit outside the van and the women showered in their own sweat. Sandstorms raged, shrouding them in red cloud. At a remote *chaikhana* (teahouse) they slept on the roof, blitzed by mosquitoes and serenaded by village dogs. Genette fell ill, and at a hostel further down the road she lay on her bed taking ice baths. By Ahwaz she was so weak Mary took her to the hospital where she was put on a drip until she slowly recovered.

From Ahwaz they drove ninety miles to Dezful, where the Khusestan Development Service were building a huge dam, and then on to Dez, climbing north out of Luristan's ravines and lightning rivers to the high rolling Kurdish upland until they reached the flat basin of Azerbaijan, in search of the Mongol's tomb. Azerbaijan's plains surround the immense salty Lake of Urmia, eighty miles long and forty wide. The lake drains all the streams from the high surrounding mountains, especially those on the west dividing Iran from Turkey. In summer the waters dry up to create great salt flats and the island of Shahi, home to the second great goal of Mary and Genette's adventure, becomes a peninsula.

'We were eager to reach Tabriz and start off our investigations of the island of Shahi, to see if there were any traces of the Mongol emperor Halugu [*sic*] on the Dadan Rock [on Shahi],' wrote Genette. 'We drove along the eastern side of the lake, but never close enough to have a good view of it; but mounting a rise we suddenly saw the big dark outline of Shahi, as big as the Channel Island of Jersey and far more mountainous. Etched against it, halfway along, sharp and clear, was the pinnacle of the Dadan Rock, clearly recognisable from the photograph at the Geographical Society. We were really excited.'

Their host at Tabriz, Sayid, agreed to drive with them for a reconnaissance towards Shahi and act as interpreter; most of the local population spoke a Turkish dialect, so the women's Persian was of no use. At a dilapidated village halfway to the island, the track they

were following died in the dust. They left the van outside the high
mud walls of a dusty courtyard and set off to find the headman. In a
formal room, covered with rough mats and a few cushions, a samovar
in the corner, Sayid told them to remain silent and respectful in the
background, 'as befitted women', while he and the headman
conferred on what possibilities there were for continuing.

'A great flap of bread was offered, too dry for us to eat more than
a mouthful. A big slice of watermelon, over which the flies
continually crawled, was also presented. Seeing us brush away the
flies, the headman produced the rush fans we had seen elsewhere in
Persia, and which are amazingly effective. We were extremely
cautious of the fly-ridden melon and ate as little as we conveniently
could.'

There was no way on to the island by vehicle, said the villagers.
The mud was too soft to support the Land-Rover. The only
alternative was to travel by foot or saddle-less camel for a round trip
of eight hours. As they discussed the predicament a tall bearded man,
his eyes concealed by dark glasses, came into the room. He said he
came from the village beneath the Dadan Rock, and would guide the
women round there by a detour of over sixty miles, where it was
possible to take the Land-Rover over the salt flats.

'This sounded better, but when he said he wanted three pounds
for this honour, we clamped down again. That was out of the
question, and no amount of bargaining could bring him down much.
Finally we decided to try this route on our own, without a guide, as
it seemed fairly clear.'

The women sped back to Tabriz, dropped Sayid at home and set
off for this north-west passage. There was no time to lose. Their visas
were soon to expire. On a minor road out of Tabriz they heard a
loud bang. One of the back tyres was flat, the first puncture for
10,000 miles and five months of Persian roads. They were distraught
to find the jack wouldn't fit under the car with the tyre so deflated,
so they had to hack a hole in the stone road with a gardening fork.
Further along the road they found a mechanic – never in short supply
along these crude roads – and paid for the tyre to be repaired.

At the village of Vaigan, the last settlement marked on the map
before the mud flats, they once again despaired at ever reaching
Shahi, the flats seemingly impassable. In the winding streets they met
a smart young man who worked in Tehran.

'I have never been to Shahi,' he said, adding after a moment's thought, 'but we could try it if you like. I would come with you.'

'We shall need to be away for a night,' said the women.

'*Taman, taman.*' No problem. He climbed in and directed them through a maze of narrow streets to his mother's house, into which he disappeared for a moment before returning with jacket in his hand. It was all he wanted for this adventure.

The Land-Rover strained over the flats. At any moment the wheels could have hit a wet patch, sink and be stranded. Genette, the driver, was sweating with fear and concentrating hard to avoid dark patches and thick salt crusts.

'Soon we were only a couple of hundred yards from the thick green tussocks which grew down the edge of the flats. But just on this last patch we could see it was wetter, and a second or so later the engine was stalling. Putting it down into low wheel ratio, I tried to pull forward, but the wheels were sticking hopelessly. I rushed it into reverse, and the heavy machine heaved its way out of the mud back onto the firm flat. It had been a nasty moment.'

When they finally came to a halt, the Dadan Rock thrust a thousand feet above them. A golden eagle circled the sky. Further up the northern coast they could see three or four houses huddled into a tiny hamlet and on their side of the rock there was an inset valley. Settling down for the night their companion slurped coffee, rolled his jacket into a pillow and tugged himself into one of the sleeping bags. He was up at dawn the next day, haggling with a shepherd for spring water, but when the women began to climb the rock he stayed behind, kicking his flat-bottomed shoes against the dust. The rock was very loose and crumbly and soon Mary decided she could go no further. Genette edged her way on slowly up the scree, testing each hand and foothold, but their hopes of finding Hulagu's tomb were waning.

'It was becoming ever more apparent that it would have been impossible to build a fortification or to carry up the coffin of an emperor and bury it on this pinnacle,' wrote Genette. 'At last I reached a lower summit and, gazing across at the peak of the main one, it was quite clear that it would be inaccessible without ropes.'

They did not give up. Five miles away was another isolated rock, rising to a similar height. It may not have matched the aerial photographs that the Royal Geographical Society had taken of what they believed to be Shahi and Hulagu's tomb, but it was more accessible. The women asked a passing shepherd what the local name of this second rock was.

'*Kale*,' he said, meaning castle. It was the Hulagu's rock. When they finally reached it, they found ancient steps cut into the side of the sheer face.

'We reached the bottom of the steps, which had been quite clearly hacked out of the rock, except in one or two places where they had fallen away, and we had to cling close to the cliff face to manoeuvre our way past. The sun was beating down relentlessly when we came up on to the open, steep, sloping stretch leading on for five hundred more feet to the summit. Halfway, we paused to look at strange slab-like shelves, about seven feet long and three wide, carved out of the rock. There were three of them, and we guessed these were the tombs of the Mongol emperor and his sons. Further up we found large rectangular water cisterns about ten feet by four feet.'

They slowly made their way to the summit, longing to explore the rest of the island but mindful of their promise to their companion to be away only one night.

'There appeared to be nothing else on the rock, but we were too hot and tired to care and it was as much as we could do to work our way down again, to the welcome shade provided by the Land-Rover, and cup after cup of lemonade. We were well satisfied that we had actually achieved the trek and climbed the rock to which, according to the villagers, no European people had at least ever been.'

First Girdkuh and now Shahi – their remarkable adventure had seen such success – but their elation would soon dissolve into fear. Over the border in Turkey lay danger, bandits, bullets, and shots in the dark.

It is eight hundred miles between the one salt lake, Urmia, and its Turkish cousin, Van. Genette and Mary headed for the border. Now familiar Farsi was useless. Everyone they encountered spoke a Turkish dialect. The border guard, however, was an exception.

'How much opium are you carrying?' he joked, inspecting their dusty grey Land-Rover.

'A couple of tons,' they quipped. It was a reminder that they would be travelling on drug-traffic roads, towards an area which required a special permit to pass through. They had no permit but decided to try their luck.

Past Dogubayazit they turned on to a narrow track. The line of hills broke into twisting passes and they came across a small circular settlement of mud-brick Kurdish houses, the villagers dressed in bright reds and oranges and yellows. Sheep and goats gathered in the shade and, almost hidden by the falling chaff, two old oxen turned the threshing wheel. Further along the road they met a student who spoke good English:

'Do not stop until you get to Van, as there are many bandits and armed robbers in these parts.'

Lake Van shone brilliantly. Pale bare mountains rode the background. The waves lapped on black polished pebbles and clouds of sandpipers and redshank billowed along the shore. At the north-east corner of the lake, flamingo, crane, avocet, stilt and shell duck gathered. The ancient town of Van, stronghold of the Urartians and home to the Armenians until Ataturk's revolution, sprang from the marsh near the lake like some great water creature, its crenulated walls a scaly stone back. After a night in Van, sleep disturbed by a cart grinding its way up a nearby track, Genette and Mary moved further down the coast to Gevas, where a little boy hiding in the dark recesses of a crumbling mosque tried to persuade the women that he was a ghost. At the shoreline they found a boat and, in their faltering Turkish, asked the owner if he would take them out to the island of Achtamar. They bargained, he agreed and suddenly it appeared that his whole family would join them; grandfather, daughter, baby and brothers climbed into the ramshackle boat.

They slipped out onto the blue green water, laden with apples, under a benign sun. In less than an hour they reached the island, on which stood the majestic red tenth-century church of King Gagik of Vaspurakan, a cruciform building with octagonal tower which was layered with biblical carvings showing lions and gazelle, prophets and pomegranates, saints and hunting scenes. All around the church lay the exquisite tombstones of early Armenian Christians.

Mary and Genette left the family making tea in the church porch and picked their way across the rocks to a secluded bay. They stripped off and dived into the cool water, the evening sun flickering gold across their naked bodies. Many minutes later they noticed a figure perched on a rock high above them – grandfather. Across the water, a police barrier blocked the road that snaked alongside the shores of Lake Van. The women felt that this would be the moment they'd be ordered to leave the area because they had no official visas. Their luck had run out, they guessed. However, after their tyres had been sprayed with insecticide, a friendly young gendarme waved them on without asking to see any documents.

They followed the mountain pass and saw small groups of men, clustered around the orange glow of a wood fire. Could these be bandits? Sure enough, when they stopped for supper, three masked horsemen, all armed with pistols, appeared by the roadside. They surrounded the Land-Rover and their leader barked questions at Mary. She smiled and introduced herself but there was no friendly reply. The horsemen trotted around the vehicle, peering through the windows. Mary was scared but she could see a shepherd on the far hillside and knew these men would not attack her while he was in view. As the horsemen pulled back to speak among themselves, Mary suggested that she and Genette quietly pack away their supper and prepare for a quick getaway. Suddenly they leapt into the vehicle, started the engine and pulled away. The horsemen chased them along the road, shouting and cursing, but the Land-Rover was too quick for them. The men disappeared into a dust cloud.

Both women were keen to put distance between themselves and the horsemen and so as darkness descended they kept moving, their eyes straining to find a track where they might safely spend the night in the Land-Rover. But tracks were rare. Suddenly Genette spotted a rough little road to the left. They swerved onto it and dipped down steeply into a cutting. Minutes after they had stopped, the full arc of a lorry's lights swept over them. Mary could feel the hairs prickling on the back of her neck. Small noises drifted through the dark. Genette had opened the back of the Land-Rover and was slipping off her shoes before getting the Land-Rover ready for bedtime when a shot rang through the air, the bullet cracking into the car.

'Stop it,' she tried to scream, 'we are tourists,' but her voice had been whittled to a whisper.

Mary, trembling with fear, struggled to slot the keys into the ignition. Genette dived onto the ground. There was a grunt from the nearby bank and another bullet whizzed past.

'Get in!'

'I've lost my shoe.'

'Leave it.'

30. Professor David Stronach presenting Geza Fehavari to the Shah of Persia

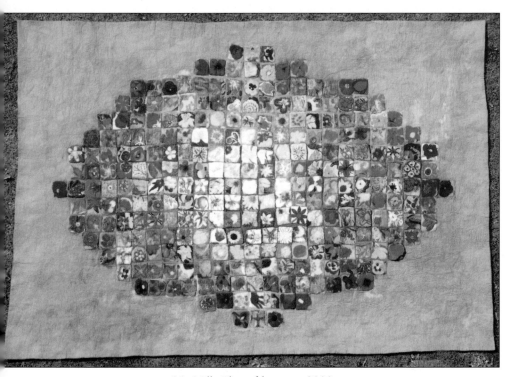

31. Mille Fleurs felt carpet, 2000

32. Genette and Mary in chadors, Meshed

33. The Shah Mosque, Isfahan

34. Tomb of Cyrus the Great, Pasargadae

35. Keramat with his mother and sister

36. Mary on top of Dadan Rock

37. Genette testing the depth of a water cistern on Dadan Rock

38. King Gagik's church, Achtamar

39. Barbara Hepworth's Trezion

40. Princess Alexandra with John Anstee at the Folk Museum, Abbot Hall

41. Eva Chew and Rosemary Cramp

42. Lord Rosse presenting Henry Moore's Moon Head *as the Museum of the Year Award, Abbot Hall, April 1973*

43. George Romney's The Gower Family, *Hugh Jenkins and Mary. Photograph courtesy of the* Westmorland Gazette

Genette leapt inside, lying flat in the back, the door open. As the Land-Rover lurched off in first gear a third bullet shot overhead. Genette was worried about Mary, sitting upright and vulnerable in the driver's seat and Mary prayed that Genette wasn't too much of an easy target. She swerved and spun the vehicle, trying to unlock the aim of their attackers. A fourth shot rang through the night. Neither woman knew if the other had been hit. Suddenly the vehicle juddered onto the main road and Mary sped onwards in search of help. A kilometre down the highway they met a lorry, packed tight with twenty-five men, all amazed to find two English girls alone in such deserted country in the dark.

'Bandits! Bandits! Bang Bang!' demonstrated the women, wildly pointing in the direction of the gunfire. The men indicated that there was a police post further down the road, and travelling for several more minutes Genette and Mary were met by a group of gendarmes, guns at the ready. An army officer jumped into the car and directed them to a house several miles away, from where he telephoned his commander. Then they were taken to Tatvan, reaching another patrol, rifles glistening in the lights of the car, a barrier dropped across the road.

'The lights of the town appeared at last and we were taken to the Kommandant's officer. We were led up long flights of stairs into his dimly lit room. To our relief he spoke a very slow, formal English, but by that time, after midnight, we were so exhausted that we could scarcely take in what he said.'

'I am sorry that my patrol shot at you, but you did not stop!'

Mary and Genette had been taken for bandits or drug smugglers and shot at by an army patrol in cold blood. In the night eyes of these Turkish soldiers, they had become the danger they'd been repeatedly warned about. Mary laughs now at the irony but at the time she was furious.

'The next day, our thoughts clearer, we wrote to the Kommandant explaining that we had been stationary many minutes when his patrol had crept up on us, and suggested it might have been better if they had asked questions first.'

Still shaken and angry, Mary and Genette were directed to the police station in a town called Bitlis, where they looked over the Land-Rover and found bullet holes beside the driver's seat and in the bonnet, realising suddenly just how close they had come to being shot. After making a full report to the police about the incident, complaining at the army's dangerous haste, they pulled away from Bitlis, on the slow journey home via Istanbul. For the next few nights they slept in hotels.

Mary and Genette reached England in October 1962, seven and a half months after they had left Ambleside, both agreeing that the trip had been exhilarating, their exploits at Girdkuh announced in *The Times*. For Mary the eastern adventure was not over. She would travel to Persia, Afghanistan, Turkey and Jordan many times. But first she would turn back on herself, to the source of her journey and the woman who had inspired much of this adventure. In 1964, after visiting her parents in the South of France, she headed for Asolo, Italy, home of Freya Stark.

She had written to Stark in 1961, describing her plans for the Persia trip and the search for Girdkuh, and in return had received an invitation to Asolo. At the station she was greeted by the gardener, who shunted her up to Stark's villa in an ancient Fiat. The sky was dark with storm clouds and the road pitted with puddles. At the villa she was met by Stark, resplendent in a flowing black, red and vermilion Arab robe.

'Oh hello,' she held out a welcoming hand. 'What a storm you have come in.'

In her diary Mary recorded the splendours of Freya's house. A wide marble staircase swept up to the guest bedroom, the floor covered in Turcoman mats. The bathroom walls were cut from a local red and black marble, the taps bright white porcelain. A silk tassel hung from the cistern and a small white china hand held the soap over the bath. Freya's study was lined with a beautiful bookcase and Persian pottery stood in carved niches. In the hall Greek, Etruscan and Roman pottery sat in a large cabinet. The library was stacked high with English classics. From Mary's window she could see thick snow on the far mountains, a green valley below, home to a rich red church, and fields flowing down to a stream in little folds and terraces.

Mary stayed for several days. At dinner on the first night she studied Stark's face – plumper than she had appeared in photographs.

'She wears her hair low over the right side of her face and has strong features, with great character in the turn of her head and the tone of her voice, which is capable also of the utmost gentleness and sympathy.'

They talked at length about Turkey and Persia. Stark was struggling to complete *Rome on the Euphrates*. 'But first I have to write an article for an American paper and they don't even seem to like what I write, as I write it,' she said.

'What is it to be on?' asked Mary.

'Anything I like.'

Mary offered to mend some of Stark's Persian pots, working quietly in one corner while Freya scribbled at some text. The talk turned to marriage.

'You must never marry for the sake of it,' said Stark. 'You must be absolutely sure. I never regret not being married now. It's in the middle years it matters, not the last ones. I did marry once – to a man who should never have married anyone, so I think we were much happier away from each other.'

At last it was time to go. It was early in the morning and Stark was sitting up in bed when Mary said goodbye. Stark thanked her profusely for taking the time to visit.

'Well, I've loved having you. Come again, any time you're in Italy. When will you be coming?'

As they kissed on both cheeks, Mary felt they'd known each other for years, not days.

Mary's love affair with the East did not end with this visit to one of its greatest explorers. In 1965 Cadogan Special Tours asked her to act as a guide for a party bound for Persia. She accepted. It was the first of many tours she lead in Persia, Turkey, Afghanistan, Syria and Jordan over the next twenty years. On each trip she was never far from an adventure – hunting for felts in a Kabul bazaar, stumbling across explorer Eric Newby and his wife Wanda in a Yemen airport, watching panic spread through the northern Afghanistan town of Mazar-i-Sherif as an eclipse blackened the sky or touring the Persian desert with Vivienne Greene, widow of Graham, on a memorable trip in 1971.

'We stayed in a lovely caravanserai,' remembers Mrs Greene. 'It was one of these that had been freshened up and there was a great big aviary. One of the pillars was leaning like the tower of Pisa. All the carvings on the walls showed people bringing gifts to the Shah.'

On the return journey to Isfahan from a newly discovered mosque at Vazarneh, the group's car ground to a halt in the desert, the wheels spinning against a mound of sand. While a tractor dragged the vehicle to safety, Mrs Greene shouted,

'Someone's dropped a pot!'

The group had stumbled onto a sixth century Sassanian site, unearthed by the shifting sands. They gathered as much pottery as they could and set off back to Isfahan, while the desert reburied its treasures, never to be found again.

CHAPTER 5

Abbot Hall

THE HISTORY OF ABBOT HALL in Kendal stretches back to Norman times, when Ivo Taillebois gave the church of Kendal and its land to the newly founded Benedictine Abbey of St Mary at York. In the Middle Ages a house was built for the Abbot on that land, a Hall which passed through the hands of illustrious Kendal families – Stirzaker, Bateman, Wood, Dixon, Harrison, and Benson – until George Wilson, a Colonel of the First Foot, knocked it down in 1759. In its place he built a new house, beautifully set among green lawns and tall trees, said to have cost £8,000 and designed (though some dispute it) by leading architect John Carr of York. After a century and a half of upper-crust ownership – tenants included Rydal Baronet Michael Le Fleming, naval surgeon John Taylor (who had made a fortune in India) and the legal luminary Sir Alan Chambre – the Hall was bought by the Kendal Corporation for £3,750. The grounds became a public park but for half a century, except for two short spells as a nursery school during the World Wars, the house was left empty.

In the early 1950s Kendal's Georgian Society launched a campaign to restore the crumbling relic and a working party, chaired by Earl Temple of Stowe, was created to explore the possibility of turning Abbot Hall into an art gallery and cultural centre. In 1957 the newly formed Lake District Art Gallery Trust bought the building, determined to reinvest the Hall with its former grandeur – as a centre for the arts.

Among the Trust's members were Robin Bagot, owner of the nearby country estate of Levens Hall; Eric Nicholson, a watercolour collector and violin expert whose playing career was halted by a hand injury; Paul Wilson, the chairman of Gilkes Engineering Works in Kendal, and Mary's friend Francis Scott. They appointed Helen Kapp the Director and Mary had been offered the post of Director's assistant before she had departed for Persia.

When Mary arrived in late 1962 locals had already begun donating works of art to Abbot Hall, including paintings by people as well

known as Ruskin and Turner. The gallery now had a staff of five –
Director Helen Kapp, her secretary, Mary, the caretaker and his wife.
By the time Mary retired on 1 June 1986 Abbot Hall had forty-five
full and part-time staff members, and the Trust managed seven
buildings: Abbot Hall itself; the Museum of Lakeland Life and
Industry, housed in the Hall's stable block; the old Kendal Grammar
School, which became a toy museum; Kendal Borough Museum,
which housed the Museum of Natural History and Archaeology; for
a time Hawkshead Courthouse, which the National Trust asked them
to run; and Stott Park Bobbin Mill, the management of which was
passed to them by the Department of the Environment.

One of Abbot Hall's earliest purchases was a Barbara Hepworth
sculpture – the swirling bronze *Trezion* that has kept pride of place
on the front lawn since its arrival. For an early assignment Mary was
dispatched to St Ives, where she was to try and coax a free sculpture
from the famously taciturn Hepworth. Mary quickly realised that the
scheme had little chance of success – buy one, get one free is not a
common offer in the art world – but she went anyway.

'I had a very pleasant time and watched her sculpt away in her little
courtyard,' remembers Mary. 'She was a bit austere but very friendly.
She talked about her work. She did intimidate me a bit. I was pretty
green then. She said she was sorry, but she couldn't give us one.
Perfectly reasonable reaction to our greedy intentions!'

In 1966 Helen Kapp retired and Peter Scott, Francis's son and
Chairman of the Trust, invited Mary to become acting Director. In
1967 she was officially appointed to the post. Her first major task was
to create a folk museum, which eventually became the Museum of
Lakeland Life and Industry. It was a good time to launch such a
venture. In those days before eBay and *The Antiques Roadshow*,
artefacts were not commonly viewed as collectibles and people were
less reluctant to give away antiques and industrial relics than they
would be today. Mary was keen to collect and display the ephemerae
of Lakeland life, ordinary objects that could tell the region's story
gathered from homes and workplaces.

A new folk museum committee was created, with Paul Wilson
(later to become Lord Wilson) at its head. Mary was sent on
reconnaissance to the Cultra craft and industry museum near Belfast,
which opened in 1964 and was already attracting over 100,000
visitors a year. She was then launched on a continental tour to collect

ideas, racing through Holland, Denmark, Sweden and Norway with a notepad and pen, impressed by how much more refined the Scandinavian folk museums were than their British counterparts. (This sophistication was a legacy, Mary believes, of the relatively slow pace of the region's industrial revolution, which allowed antiquarians and curators more time to translate tools from obscurity to posterity.) In Stockholm's Skansen museum she found reconstructed houses where potters and silversmiths worked, plus a zoo, restaurant, concert hall and theatre. At Lillehammer in Norway, where a simple concrete building contained a maze of displays, spatial disorientation lent itself to temporal confusion and visitors found it easier to imagine standing within the wattle and daub of a Viking smithy.

Mary did not want to copy the exhibitions; longships were never built in Kendal. 'But you could pick up ideas on the use of light, the use of space, the contrasts of objects, the aesthetics of objects, the relevance of a certain craft to the area and the use of materials that would make the display more convincing. There were all sorts of techniques that you could look at, understand for the first time and apply to our building.'

When she and John Anstee designed the Kendal museum Mary tried hard to create an evocative atmosphere with lighting, props, sounds and smells. They recorded local characters, such as a Kendal pig farmer and an Ambleside cobbler, and played the tapes through speakers in three different sections of the museum. Olive Rummens, secretary to both Helen Kapp and later Mary, remembers:

'We used to go out to a peat farm south of Kendal and she recorded these wonderful Westmorland peat diggers. She could get them to pour out their life onto a tape.'

Mary was careful not to let the sounds overlap. Other innovations were not so successful. The lavender placed in the Victorian bedroom was no match for the manure dumped in the farming section, the stench of which skulked through the building until it had to be removed.

In their lunch hour Mary and Olive Rummens would rush down to the riverbank, site of the Roman fort at Kendal, and search for pieces of pottery. Since the site sat opposite the Kendal sewer it was not the best place to have a picnic, but the women did find some interesting items, which were put on display in the Kendal Museum of Natural History and Archaeology.

Olive's predecessor was Sarah Bryant, equally praised by Mary, as is John Anstee, who joined the Abbot Hall team from the Museum of Rural Life at Reading. Anstee helped design the rooms. 'He was fantastic . . . innovative, unusual, very hard-working, imaginative, brilliant at forging metal and making swords and things,' says Mary. Another valued colleague was Eva Chew, development officer in the 1970s. Eva lived at Troutbeck and Mary met her just after her husband had died. The pair would enjoy twilight badger-spotting walks. Eva's son Tony became a conspirator in Mary's stone hunts.

The museum enjoyed a varied patronage. Ann Hull-Grundy, the aged heiress to the Corgi toy fortune and a great collector of costume jewels, was an early and enthusiastic donor. Housebound with her husband (and a team of nurses) in a Hampshire mansion, Hull-Grundy was a legendarily generous patron of the arts. When Mary wrote to her saying Abbot Hall would like a share of her largesse she quickly replied, suggesting that the Lake District was good for nothing but sheep and climbers, and both would come in and spoil the museum's floors.

'So I wrote back and said there were other people in the Lake District apart from climbers and if they came in I told them to take their boots off. The sheep didn't bother to come in.'

Wonderful parcels started to arrive and a long-distance relationship based on humour and a shared love of beautiful objects developed. Mrs Hull-Grundy would send up jet necklaces, gold rings, coral bracelets and Victorian brooches. In return she asked only for the postage to be paid and for museums to publish proper catalogues – and once she requested that Mary send some Stonecrop for her pet pigeons. It was a good bargain and Mary kept her side of it, even on the occasions when Mrs Hull-Grundy was less than polite.

'She could be frightfully rude to me. She would call me a lazy old cow. But I took absolutely no notice of her because that was the way she was with everybody. In spite of the fact that she was an invalid and her husband was an invalid, and they lived alone in Hampshire, she had the whole world at the bedside.

'We had contemplated meeting but both she and I on the telephone said perhaps we'd be a disappointment. She used to describe herself lying in bed with her ermine stole. She told wonderful stories of her childhood. She had been sent to Cheltenham [Ladies College] and she told me this lovely tale about how she had nearly been expelled because she had been dancing in the moonlight with her other little girlfriends, naked. On another occasion she had forged her father's handwriting to ensure early release from school. She had passed all her exams and been bored.'

When Ann Hull-Grundy died there were no more parcels, but the museum had a splendid memorial in her generous gifts (which included an Epstein).

The hard work of Mary and her team paid off. In April 1971, Princess Alexandra officially opened the Museum Of Lakeland Life and Industry, which won the first ever Museum of the Year Award. From a shortlist of six, the judges had picked it out for singular praise because of its originality and flair. First prize was £1,000 and a year's possession of Henry Moore's *Moon Head* sculpture, worth considerably more. The award ceremony was televised on BBC2's *Chronicle* programme. Mary was delighted at the success. It was not the last she would hear about the awards. In 1977 she became a judge for the Museum of the Year Award in Scotland and in 1986 for England and Wales, travelling from one museum to the next, looking for the same qualities that led to Abbot Hall's success in 1973.

Mary was continually amazed by the generosity of local people towards the gallery and museum. A Friends of Abbot Hall scheme was launched in 1963, which attracted 1,300 members by the time she retired. Their donations helped the gallery continue to build its collection. Assistance came from other quarters in the unlikely figure of Roy Nicholson, Cumbrian officer for Northern Arts. Roy, resplendent in flared jeans and seventies moustache, took Mary's requests for funding seriously. He sat up late with her at his Skelton home, enthusing about the arts after dinner, his wife complaining that she'd lost them to a world of painters, commissions and visitors' books.

Throughout her time at Abbot Hall, Mary continued to build the permanent collection. She was often invited by local families to view paintings or antiques, either as an independent eye, potential recipient or buyer for Abbot Hall. There were pleasant surprises hoarded in Lake District homes, including a fifteenth-century prayer book with eight illuminated original illustrations, which earned the owner several thousand pounds in a Sotheby's sale. Another friend of the gallery offered Abbot Hall a peculiar wooden object discovered in a seventeenth-century desk. It was an early calculator and too important to be given to her museum. It was eventually housed in the National Museum in Edinburgh.

Perhaps the most exciting of Mary's finds was a Burmese temple carving discovered in a Lake District farm, bought at Broughton Market near Cockermouth. The owner had been a prisoner of war in Burma and had studied Burmese art. Again Mary contacted a curator, this time the head of the Oriental Museum in Durham. When the gift was agreed the carving had to be piled onto a tractor-trailer piece by piece, carried over a snow-smothered field towards a waiting van.

Exhibitions at Abbot Hall sometimes reflected Mary's interests, sometimes the interests of Lakeland collectors or artists. In 1966 the gallery mounted a popular Beatrix Potter exhibition. It was followed by 'A Thousand Years of Persian Art', opened by the Persian Ambassador to Britain and running from September to November 1967. In 1970, on the 150th anniversary of the birth of artist, critic and Lakes lover John Ruskin, Abbot Hall held a major exhibition of his work.

Come September 1971 eastern wonder was again woven within the walls of Abbot Hall as the Turcoman came to Kendal. A fully furnished Turcoman tent was erected in the large upper gallery of Abbot Hall, containing the household objects of a typical Turcoman family. Turcoman music was played quietly inside, spellbinding children who stepped into the tent to investigate.

The list of exhibitions slips on and on, and all the time the permanent collection grew.

A lecture season began at Abbot Hall, the first invitation extended to Roy Strong, then head of the Victoria and Albert and later Director of the National Portrait Gallery. Mary and Strong bartered like buyers at a bazaar.

'Now if you were to offer me three different lectures at different places, with a couple of visits to stately homes thrown in, I'd come,' he said.

'Done,' she replied, swiftly arranging for him to speak at Preston and Carlisle art galleries, and to visit Levens Hall and Skipton Castle. Afterwards she had only to mention that Sir Roy had been her guest and other national museum and gallery directors were loath to refuse. Nikolaus Pevsner was another heavyweight of the art world tempted north. As chair of the Keswick group of the National Association of

Decorative and Fine Arts, Mary invited the famous architectural historian to deliver a lecture. He agreed, pacing back and forth across the platform as he spoke in measured and solemn tones.

'I think he was rather shy of women,' she recalls. 'But I found him very friendly and very easy to get on with.'

At Christmas 1973 a rare opportunity for the gallery arose – the purchase of the neo-classical Gower Family painting by Lakeland master George Romney. Romney died in Kendal in 1802. He was born in south Cumbria's Dalton in Furness, moved to London in 1762 but returned to Cumbria three years before his death.

The Gower Family's owner was Bond Street's Leger Gallery. Director David Posnett, like many British art lovers, didn't want this important piece to be shipped abroad. The painting would be Abbot Hall's most ambitious purchase to date and did not meet with universal approval. There were mutterings among the committee about the £300,000 price tag. Posnett was prepared to reduce the cost to £210,000 but it was only with the help of a long list of benefactors – including the Victoria and Albert Museum Grant-in-aid-Fund, the Government, Westmorland County Council, the National Art-Collections Fund, The Provincial Insurance PLC, various private donors and the Friends of Abbot Hall – that *The Gower Family* came to Kendal. The *Guardian*, *Daily Telegraph* and *The Times* hailed the purchase as a triumph for British art.

Mary's negotiations on obtaining the £20,000 government grant, conducted by telephone with Westminster mandarin Norman St John Stevas, were accompanied by the clink of bedpans. She had broken her hip in a car accident and was speaking to him lying down, her leg raised and covered in plaster, in a Kendal hospital ward. She had been driving home on the particularly frosty evening of 17 November 1973 after a late meeting with the Borough Council, when she fell asleep at the wheel and swerved into an oncoming Mini. Luckily the other driver, alone in his car, was not hurt but Mary had broken her hip and was now trapped in her crushed vehicle. As a woman in a nearby house called for an ambulance, a passing motorist asked Mary, now uncommonly taciturn, again and again for the number of somebody he could contact to tell about the crash. Mary thought he was testing her memory, trying to gauge if she had suffered a head injury, so she reeled off a long list of names and numbers. She was admitted to a general ward and soon inundated with visitors, her young helper having contacted everyone she had mentioned. (One of these visitors was a gravedigger whom Mary had met while searching for Roman artefacts at the Kendal archaeological site. Mary's friend Olive Wilson thought his appearance was hilarious, joking that although the accident was serious he was being a bit premature.) Mary was kept in hospital for ten weeks, attended every day by her secretary Joyce Harvey. She was determined to run Abbot Hall from her bed, surrounded that 1972 Christmas by well wishers' cards. Eventually the hip healed, although the injury was to plague her later in life, and Mary returned to Abbot Hall.

The Gower Family was the largest but not the only prestigious work housed in the gallery. The 1977 catalogue is rich in great painting, drawings and sculpture and includes works by national icons like William Blake and John Constable, as well as local artists like Wordsworth's friend William Green and the prolific John Harden. Over thirty different watercolours and drawings by John Ruskin are listed, most given in 1973 by the local Barton family. Among the oils are Hilde Goldschmidt's *Self-portrait*, Patrick Heron's *Red Painting*, five other Romney works, *A Fellow Internee* by Kurt Schwitters, plus a 1944 still life of his, and work by Cumbrian Sheila Fell.

Richard Long was one of several 'celebrities' whom Mary invited to open exhibitions and help publicise the gallery and museum. Born in Bristol in 1945, Long studied at the West of England College of Art in Bristol and at St Martin's School of Art in London. In the early 1960s he began to create landscape sculptures, an art form that would become his trademark. He has made sculptures by walking, hitchhiking or bicycling in circles and straight lines, recording these expeditions as maps, photographs and short, descriptive texts. He has travelled the world for his work, splashing Amazonian mud in controlled sweeps across a gallery in Sao Paulo to form one of his most celebrated works, creating outdoor evanescent sculptures, of leaves or sticks, and more permanent works, such as the Six Stone Circles he laid with Delabole slate from a Cornish quarry in a private garden at Kingston-on-Thames. In 1989 Long won the Turner Prize.

His visit, during which he exhibited some of his work and left a handprint on the wall (later accidentally blocked off), followed that of Patrick Heron, whose modern experiments with colour on canvas had earned him an international reputation. L. S. Lowry, the Salford industrial painter famous for his 'matchstick' men and women, was another visitor, opening an exhibition of his paintings at Abbot Hall.

'One knows that he was shy and never married, but we got on very well. He didn't show his shyness. He didn't have many friends among women.'

Lowry was something of an eccentric; accepting an invitation to Mary's house-warming party in Grasmere and then creeping across to Eleanor Calthrop's door as soon as he had arrived because he 'didn't like parties'; falling asleep in his dinner at Peter Scott's home at Longdales; riding in a taxi from Manchester to the Aspatria home of his protégée Sheila Fell in his bedroom slippers.

Mary is an admirer of Sheila Fell. In the late nineties she helped raise £1,250 for a plaque, now hanging on Aspatria's Methodist Church commemorating Fell's work. The town council's Margaret Dunglinson suggested that if Mary raised £100 the council would match the money. A meagre £200 wouldn't go far on a plaque, Mary thought, and it was eventually agreed that if the council gave £250 she would raise £1,000. After eight phone calls to fellow Fell fans (who have requested anonymity) Mary had her £1,000.

In March 1968 Mary organised the first of several exhibitions of Lucie Rie's work at Abbot Hall. Rie was born in Vienna in 1902 and at the age of twenty studied ceramics at the Kunstgewerbeschule under Michael Powolny. In 1926 she married hat manufacturer Hans Rie and spent eleven years working at the wheel in their apartment, producing elegant earthenware. In 1938 the couple fled to England as refugees from fascism, although the marriage was dissolved two years later when Hans settled in America. Rie took a small house in Albion Mews near Hyde Park where she lived until her death in April 1995. By the end of the war she had specialised in making ceramic jewellery and porcelain buttons, but by 1946 she was back at the wheel developing an influential working relationship with the young German refugee Hans Coper, whose giant candleholders set a world record price for a contemporary ceramic, taking £88,000 at auction. Although Rie was able to find buyers for her tableware and exhibitors for her porcelain and stoneware throughout the fifties and sixties, as well as time to develop new glazes and clays that led to more idiosyncratic work, it was not until the late sixties that she came to the attention of the art establishment. In 1967 the Arts Council organised a 300-piece retrospective exhibition of her work and in

1968 she was awarded the OBE. In 1991 she was made a Dame of the British Empire.

Whenever Mary visited London she would take tea with Rie in her little house at Albion Mews.

'She was very gentle, small, frail, mid-European, with a quiet voice, a charming smile, very reserved. She loved her little garden. In front of the house was a huge creeper. The studio was downstairs. This little spiral staircase led up to her living room, kitchen and bedroom. Inside it was all white walls and low shelves, on which she kept her pots. There was a low chair she sat in. Grey squirrels used to come and eat the feed she'd put out for them.'

One of Rie's greatest patrons was the naturalist and broadcaster David Attenborough, whose short film about Rie saw him pulling the octogenarian out of her top-loading kiln by her legs after she had tumbled in its mouth while trying to lift a large pot. Attenborough himself was a regular visitor to Abbot Hall. His aunt, a Mrs Peaker who lived at Grasmere, had explained to Mary that David's love of natural history had sprouted on trips to the Lake District. Mary wrote to him and secured his services for publicity. He visited her house, Demavend, and they spent one afternoon shopping for lace bobbins along Kendal High Street.

'He was great fun, very knowledgeable and very amusing.'

David Bellamy was another naturalist persuaded to lend a hand. After officially opening a show at the Kendal Museum of Archaeology and Natural History in October 1981, he and Mary took local schoolchildren down to the river to search for small fish and water larvae. The outing was unfortunately cut short when one small boy decided to throw a stone at one of his fellow students. There was some screaming but no permanent damage. When Professor Bellamy visited Mary at Isel Hall with his family, she took them to lunch at the Ghyll Yat pub in nearby Blindcrake. The owners had moved in that day and were still unpacking.

'All they had were crisps and drink. So we sat and drank and ate crisps till we were woozy. Then they came back here and ate cake, because that's all *I* had.'

Other guests were more regal than the down-to-earth Bellamy. In 1984 Mary planned an exhibition of Jordanian tribal art and culture. She invited King Hussein to be guest of honour at the grand opening. He was willing but a domestic crisis scuppered the plan. His daughter

Princess Alia arrived instead. She stayed at Bowness's Old England hotel with her lady-in-waiting, the local press in rapture over such an exotic visitor.

When another exhibition of Jordanian art opened in Liverpool the city gallery director Richard Foster invited Mary to attend the ceremony, presided over by Alia's stepmother, Queen Noor. Mary's train was late and she ran up the gallery steps, through the entrance and into the great hall to see all the staff lined up waiting for the Queen. Richard Foster roared with laughter and said, 'Oh, it's you we're waiting for, is it, Mary?'

'I dashed and put my hat on and put away my plastic bag in which I had taken my other shoes, and went and stood at the back of the reception committee. To my horror Queen Noor came in and we were wearing exactly the same coloured suits. I wanted to go down under the floor. I felt like disappearing.'

Mary was equally nervous meeting the Queen Mother at the opening of the 1976 Islamic Festival in the Science Museum, London. In fact a lively conversation about Persian monuments sprang up between her and the elderly royal, and Mary was ushered away by Lord Carrington after spending so long with the 'precious' guest, only to be confronted by the Queen of Persia, the *Shahbanou*, who had personally donated money to Abbot Hall for the Qashqai exhibition they had mounted in 1976.

'I was able to talk to her because I could thank her for the help she'd given over the exhibition and she was very nice, but much harder to talk to than the Queen Mum, who was simply wonderful.'

A dinner she attended with the Queen Mother's son-in-law did not go quite so smoothly. She shot her food at him, poking at a hard little new potato that jumped straight over onto Prince Philip's plate, skidded onto his knee and plopped onto the floor.

'It wasn't a good start. The butler came around and kicked it deftly up to the other end of the table, where he retrieved it.'

When Mary met Prince Charles, at the opening of a nature reserve at Threlkeld, Cumbria, it was the turn of her friend, Patrick Gordon-Duff-Pennington, owner of the Cumbrian coast's Muncaster Castle, to embarrass her. He introduced her as 'the maddest woman in Cumbria, a stone-collector who dashes off to Afghanistan and other strange lands'.

'How do you start a conversation after that?' asked the Prince.

Princess Alexandra officially opened the Museum of Lakeland Life and Industry in 1971 and Mary met her a second time when she received an honorary degree from Lancaster University in December 1997, having almost missed the ceremony. The roads were covered in ice that morning and Mary decided to leave her car at home and take the train. She drove to Penrith station, where she discovered that her train was cancelled. The replacement service ran straight to Preston without stopping, so a taxi was hailed to Lancaster. Mary arrived at the university just in time to be led into lunch by robed graduates, breathlessly explaining her troubled journey to the Princess.

Despite this particular setback Mary has fond memories of Cumbrian railway stations – unsurprisingly, since she enjoyed rather personal service. From Oxenholme, the nearest mainline station to Kendal, she would take the train to London once or twice a week. When she arrived late she would 'dash in and I remember once handing my car keys to someone whom I thought was the new porter, because he had a cap and a uniform, and I said, "Park the car. I'm going to miss the train." I jumped onto the train and went to London. When I got back the porters were standing on the platform and one said, "You gave the keys to a driver, a train driver, and he wouldn't take his train on to Glasgow until he'd parked your car."'

On the day she explained to the porters that she was worried about the car's spluttering engine, she returned to find that they had changed the fan belt and cleaned the spark plugs.

When Mary arrived back in the Lake District after her Persian adventure, she bought a small flat in Ambleside that soon turned out to be 'insufferably damp'. On the advice of her doctor she temporarily moved into his house, and six months later her friend Eleanor Calthrop offered her the cottage in Grasmere. Mary enjoyed the company and evenings chatting over dinner, but the tourists blocked the roads in summer and the drive to Kendal took fifty minutes in high season. So Mary decided to buy some land from the Scotts in Bowness and have her own house built. Named Demavend after the Persian mountain, it is a wood structure of Scandinavian design, roof stretching down to the ground, an isosceles triangle of a building.

A picture of the Demavend house, Mary standing at the doorway, hangs on the kitchen wall at her present home, Isel Hall. It is a pen and ink drawing by Alfred Wainwright, the celebrated author, artist and television presenter who poured his passion for the Lakes into a series of best-selling books. Wainwright gave the picture to Mary as a present. She came into regular contact with Wainwright working at Abbot Hall. He was Kendal Borough Treasurer and an honorary curator of Kendal Museum. At ten o'clock on Monday morning they would meet in the Town Hall to discuss the museum's finances. At first Mary found Wainwright quite stern, insisting on being called Mr Wainwright, rarely smiling and waving his pipe to emphasise his speech. Gradually, however, a friendship developed.

'We talked strictly about the matters in hand but then he began to get quite warm towards me. He was a retiring person, but I like retiring people because it's really rather nice to see then unfurling.' Wainwright explained his fascination with the Lakes and soon revealed his passion for Roman archaeology. He was keen to visit the Roman fort at Hardknott, west of Ambleside.

'He hadn't got a car and he couldn't drive so I asked if he would like me to take him with me [to the fort]. He was a huge man and I had a very small car in those days. I remember bundling him into the car and he just about fitted in.'

Wainwright was fascinated by Hardknott and grateful for Mary's kindness. She offered him lifts to the starting points of other walks when she had time. In 1966 she was due to spend a weekend in Sheffield with her friend Dr May Beattie, an expert in carpets who had studied in Iraq. Wainwright was working on the *Pennine Way Companion* at the time and he wanted to get down to Derbyshire. Mary offered to drop him off en route and pick him up two days later on her return from Sheffield. Wainwright gratefully accepted. The pair decided to spend the return night in Buxton. Wainwright booked separate rooms at a hotel for them.

'I had a bad headache and went to bed early. When I came down in the morning I had breakfast and then went to pay my bill. The receptionist told me that the gentleman had paid my bill.'

Mary blushed, thinking the cashier was probably reading more into the situation than was necessary. Wainwright, standing nearby with a cautious smile, blushed too but he was just trying to thank Mary in kind for driving. They had kept to their separate rooms.

When she drove him to the Roman fort at Ravenglass on the west coast of Cumbria in April 1969. Wainwright wandered around the site with gleeful curiosity, stopping only to watch astonished as Mary took his photograph. He was camera-shy, she explains – a strange trait for a man who became an early television star.

Hunter Davies, another literary lover of Lakeland, wrote about their friendship in his biography of Wainwright, as part of a chapter entitled 'Wainwright and His Women'. There had been rumours in Kendal about the pair, especially after Mary drove Wainwright down to Buxton, but Mary insists that the relationship remained platonic. Wainwright did however confide in Mary about the problems with his marriage. He said he lived in one room of his Kendal Green house and his wife Ruth lived in another. The cat, but no words, passed between them.

'I did once go to Kendal Green, on business, and was given coffee,' Mary told Davies. 'Ruth stayed in the next room and I never met her. I always found him funny, in a dry sort of way. I can still hear him saying, "Did you take that photo?" That still makes me laugh. The younger generation didn't find him funny. To them he was very formal and retiring. He *was* retiring, oh goodness. I never ever managed to get him to turn up to any openings, of his exhibitions or anyone else's.

'When he fell out with people – that was it. He was never mealy-mouthed. He saw things in black and white. "People annoy me" he used to say. "You can't go wrong with animals." He hated modern art, so we kept off that subject, and we didn't discuss cats.' Mary the ornithologist hates bird-killing cats.

In 1983 Wainwright gave Abbot Hall the licence to publish his book *Wainwright in Lakeland*, dedicated to Francis Scott, and to keep the profits. The gallery made £15,000. During Mary's tenure Abbot Hall staged three exhibitions of Wainwright's work, not always to local acclaim, despite his technical prowess.

He was one of a multitude of artists whom Mary helped promote. Some, like Richard Long, hardly needed the exposure. Mary gave other less well-known painters or sculptors a first chance to display their wares to the world. Jenny Cowern was one of them.

'In about 1977 or 1978 I took a car load of paintings down to Abbot Hall to show the Director Mary Burkett,' wrote Cowern, 'hoping to get my first exhibition since leaving the RCA (Royal College of Art) in 1966. It was quite a daunting meeting, but an exhibition was agreed for late 1979 and was to be of paintings from the previous ten years' work.'

After the exhibition Jenny took time to view the Feltmakers' exhibition at Abbot Hall, which accompanied Mary's book.

'The effect of seeing this wonderfully energetic and patterned exhibition was to at once abandon pattern and to throw myself into learning how to dye wool to make colours which could be used by a painter; to experiment with making felt (made possible by descriptions in the catalogue/book by M.E.B); and to make numerous direct studies of skies in drawing and colour media as reference.

'I remember Miss Burkett seeing them, and though I cannot know exactly what she thought she appeared to question what they were, because they were so different from the felts she knew so much about. I had lifted a technique and used it like painting, and I had to convince her that the technique was exactly as I had learned from her research. This first exhibition, and the introduction to felt, both thanks to her, gave me the impetus to go forward both in production of new work and in finding venues to exhibit.'

When the Theatre By The Lake opened in Keswick in 1998 an entire floor was given over to Jenny Cowern's felt 'paintings'.

In the mid eighties, under Mary's auspices, sculptor Edward Allington exhibited at Abbot Hall. The pair had been friends for many years. They met in 1958 when Edward was seven and a pupil at Calgarth Primary School near Windermere. Allington eloquently explains:

'My mother was a Jehovah's Witness, which made me a sort of outcast. As the Witnesses were not recognized as Christians I seemed to be categorised as some sort of pagan – an idea I found rather exciting even though I didn't really understand why, as my mother insisted we were true Christians.

'I went with her door-to-door spreading the "truth". I read copies of their literature, illustrated with extraordinary images of biblical stories and people in suits and skirts sitting in fields with lions and other animals. My father was a plumber and not a Witness, an unpredictable man given to fantasies of Aryan supremacy, who thought it reasonable to dress his children in German national costume. It was not a happy household when he was present.

'I did not like school and was not doing well there. I remember having to fight a lot, either about the religion I was supposed to belong to or for being a German. Then one day we had a visit from a teacher from outside the school who brought lots of amazing things

into the classroom – real Roman things which she had dug from the
ground. Not the ground from some faraway place which could be
pointed out on a map, but the ground around where we lived. Thus
I met Miss Burkett. She remembers me as a small blond-haired boy
with big feet. I remember a table with incredible things on it and a
kind person who actually answered my questions, didn't hit me, tell
me I was stupid or tell me to go away.'

After Allington expressed such irrepressible fascination in her
Roman artefacts, Mary asked his parents if she could take him on one
of the digs she was working on.

'It still amazes me that my father let me go, although knowing Miss
Burkett, I imagine she phrased the request in such a way that my father
had less choice in the matter than he thought he had. I found myself
high in the fells at Hardknott, a Roman fort. I remember being given a
small trowel and a brush and shown how to gently move the earth and
how to look for small objects. I was allowed to keep the things I
found, contorted rusted shapes I was told were once Roman nails, and
fragments of red pottery. These were things of no archaeological
significance. To me they were treasures. I have them still.

'Did I go there just once? I cannot remember, but I remember the
shape of the hills, the sky above me, her encouragement and
boundless enthusiasm. I remember sitting with other people working
at the dig and eating my sandwiches. I remember a man who told me
about how he had tried to see a ghost, how he had slept in haunted
houses and graveyards, but had not seen one yet. My mother had
impressed on me that ghosts did exist, that she had experienced their
presence and how they were the work of the devil. I think I returned
from that trip with the sense that there was a different type of truth
to the one I lived in.

'I remember a visit to Miss Burkett's house . . . We talked and she
showed me some more wonderful things, gave me a stone axe head
from Langdale and some stones, one of which was a fossil. Yes, I have
these still. Thus I learned about the power of objects, not only their
formal presence but also the beauty of the ideas they embodied.
History became alive to me and has remained so. The fossil was of
particular significance. The Jehovah's Witnesses maintain a funda-
mentalist viewpoint. The concept of evolution is anathema to them.
It was not the things themselves that did this. It was the way Miss
Burkett animated them, told their story.

'Of course, all this did not happen at once, in the moment or the year I was seven. It was the beginning. I had someone who would listen to my questions and answer them, although what questions I asked then are lost to me now.'

In August 1998 Mary assisted with an exhibition of Kurt Schwitters's work at the Hatton Gallery in Newcastle University, the fruit of forty years of fervour for Schwitters, one of the leading figures in early twentieth-century German art whose paintings now hang in galleries across Europe. Born in Hanover in 1887, Schwitters studied for six years at the Academy in Dresden and at the Royal Gymnasium. He was influenced by Kandinsky and Franz Marc, by Picasso and Cubism, and between 1923–32 collaborated with fellow modernists Arp, Mondrian, Lissitzky and Von Doesburg. Schwitters is most famous for his Merzbaus, huge wall sculptures in which were plastered the detritus of modern living – old watering cans and paper wrappers, newspaper texts and pieces of lace. His first Merzbau eventually spread over three storeys of his house.

'He showed in it that everything had a purpose, nothing was wasted. The most trivial and commonplace article could have meaning if used in the right way,' wrote Mary. In this sense his art was revolutionary, a crumpled calling card to a future aesthetic in which the sculptor's search for a medium is a free-for-all.

Schwitters's first Merzbau was destroyed when the British bombed Hanover. He soon fled Germany for Norway (leaving behind his wife, who would die in 1945) and in the town of Lysaker created a second Merzbau, which was promptly set alight by vandals. From Norway he sailed for England, shrouded with depression (he'd tried to commit suicide) and on arrival was quickly dispatched to Hutchinson Square camp in Douglas on the Isle of Man. Here he was allowed to paint on panels and scraps of lino and to lecture.

In 1958, in the Art Exhibition of Brussels 'Expo', Mary stood reading her catalogue and discovered that Schwitters had died in Ambleside. She had no idea that an artist of his stature had spent his last few years in her hometown. On returning to the Lake District she began to investigate. No one had heard of Schwitters. In vain she searched Ambleside for anybody who had met the artist. Finally she discovered Harry Pierce, a former friend of the émigré who lived at Langdale near Elterwater, a short bus-ride from Ambleside:

'He was a great artist and a good man,' Pierce told Mary. 'He was so quiet and grateful for what I could give him, and, above all, so kind. He could not bear suffering, and even smuggled some white mice with him in his clothes so that they would not have to be left behind to Hitler.'

In 1941, Mary discovered, Schwitters was released from Hutchinson Square camp and moved to London. He suffered a stroke and from 1943 onwards took holidays at Ambleside in an attempt to improve his health, alongside his friend Edith Thomas. Edith had been working as a decoder and war department telephonist when they had met as fellow lodgers in a Bayswater boarding house and she had her own good reasons for escaping up to the Lakes. She'd suffered a nervous breakdown thanks to the Blitz bombing. He nicknamed her Wantee and she called the gangly German Jumbo.

In the summer of 1945 Schwitters decided to settle in Cumbria. The Museum of Modern Art in New York gave him a grant to undertake a third Merzbau. The kindly Mr Pierce allowed the artist to use an old barn in the grounds of his 'Cylinders Farm' as the 'canvas' for his work. Schwitters began to plaster tickets and papers, farmyard tools and local stones, a rubber ball and a china egg onto a wall of the barn. The Merzbau was never finished. Schwitters died in January 1948, aged 60, on a Kendal hospital ward.

After finding Mr Pierce, Mary's next task was to trace Schwitters's grave. She discovered it in St Mary's churchyard, Ambleside.

'This was not so easy as one might have thought,' wrote Mary. 'There is no stone. The verger scratched his head thoughtfully and said: "It's a long time ago." He took a dusty book from the shelf and together we counted the green sods in a long row and found the one where Kurt Schwitters was buried – no stone – and no word of remembrance.'

Mary's search for Schwitters took a personal turn. When she bought the damp flat on the Gale which climbs up out of Ambleside in 1963, she had no idea that Schwitters had lived and painted in it. Eventually, just like her, he had been driven by the damp to move down into the village. There he painted portraits of friends, landscapes and crumbling Lakeland cottages, selling them at low prices to meet the costs of daily living. As her research continued she stumbled upon the one person who could shine the most light on this remarkable artist – Wantee. Edith Thomas helped Mary piece together the missing fragments of Schwitters's life and complete the picture of a prophetic man.

'I know well that the time will come for me and all other important personalities of the abstract movement, when we will influence an entire generation,' he wrote in 1931. 'However, I fear that I shall not experience this.'

In return for their services, Schwitters had exchanged many paintings with Langdale and Ambleside people – from the local taxi driver and the dentist to the blacksmith who let him dry canvasses on the smithy floor. Much of the work remained in the Lake District after his death and so Mary decided to mount a Schwitters exhibition at Abbot Hall, under the guidance of Edith Thomas. The paintings' owners were remarkably willing to lend them for public view, even though the price of Schwitters's work was rising rapidly. Several London dealers travelled north with blank cheques and orders to buy wholesale, but to no avail. Owners were ready to lend but not to sell.

At another time and in another place, says Mary, funds would have been available to create a Schwitters centre at Elterwater, but over twenty years after the end of the Second World War people would still have been uncomfortable about commemorating a German artist, even one who saved little white mice from Adolf Hitler.

In most conversations that I have had with those who have met Mary, the word enthusiasm is mentioned – enthusiasm for paintings, for artists, for old pots, for photographs or birds, countries or friends, enthusiasm that is inspirational or irritating, energies that spin you like a top or tire you. Mary's curriculum vitae is cluttered with the extracurricular, noting Mary's membership of the Royal Geographical Society, the Museums Association, Cumbria College of Art and Design Governors, Guild of Lakeland Craftsmen, Board of Border Television, Royal Society of Arts . . . to name a few. It was her work at Abbot Hall, however, that prompted a welcome pat on the back from the Establishment in 1978 when Mary was awarded an OBE in the New Year's Honours list. She travelled down to Buckingham Palace with her sister and her niece for the ceremony. Although it was one of the proudest moments of her life, she doesn't remember much about it . . . except that 'Ronnies Barker and Corbett were there' and she met 'a very nice motorcyclist called Barry Sheen'.

She has far clearer memories, however, of her evening art class at Cumbria's Bela Prison, a task for which she volunteered with typical enthusiasm. In a low hut classroom, in the middle of which stood an anthracite stove belching vicious fumes, she attempted to teach a group of petty criminals the finer points of art. Mary made a point of leaving her purse on the table while she disappeared for her tea break – wanting 'to encourage and trust' – and not prying into her pupils' pasts.

The class grew and the students became more passionate about their art. Friendships developed and prisoners often talked about what they wanted to happen when they went home. Dispatched (by coincidence) as a work-gang to demolish a building beside Abbot Hall, they were delighted to find Mary in the middle of her working week and pleased by a surreptitious present of cigarettes from the caretaker.

'They used to paint extremely well,' says Mary. 'At first they weren't very excited but they got quite keen and showed all sorts of states of mind. One was very enthusiastic . . . and spent a lot of time painting a hill, a long limestone hill that you can see well from Bela, called Farleton Knot. It's just eroded limestone and gravelly and there's very little vegetation on it, but it goes into lovely colours according to the light, blue in colour and pink in the sunset, and it is a very romantic thing to paint.'

On the day that Mary arrived to discover that the paint cupboard had been broken open, it wasn't hard to find the culprit – her keen student, a professional burglar, had needed some more white to catch the sunset striking over Farleton Knot.

CHAPTER 6

The Writer

'Fʀᴏᴍ ʟᴀᴛᴇ ᴄʜɪʟᴅʜᴏᴏᴅ ɪ'ᴅ secretly wanted to write,' says Mary, 'but was deterred by various people saying: "What would you write about? You've got to **know** something?" . . . Then at Abbot Hall I realised that so many Lake District artists in the past had never even been recorded, let alone written about.' She had found something she did know about – the esoteric, enervating and uncharted landscape of Cumbrian art.

'My books are not creative novels, they . . . are recording people's lives. I wanted to put these artists on the map.'

The first artist to benefit from Mary's literary cartography was John Bracken, an unknown painter she first encountered in 1956 when Bracken's name appeared among entries in the accounts of Sir Daniel Fleming, seventeenth-century owner of Westmorland country pile, Rydal Hall. The ledgers recorded payments to J. Bracken for paintings of Fleming family members and various frames.

A Kirkby Stephen man, Bracken's exact date of birth is not known but it is thought he was born in 1640 and died aged 80. In middle age he moved with his son to London, where the pair were employed by the Barber-Surgeons Company. Bracken became a painter of repute. In 1974 National Portrait Gallery director Sir Roy Strong confirmed that Bracken was the author of a portrait found at Rydal of the famous Lady Anne Clifford – Elizabethan beauty, daughter of the 3rd Earl of Cumberland, early protagonist for women's rights and restorer of castles who was 'able to discourse of all things, from predestination to slea-silk' (according to John Donne). In fact, as Mary discovered, Bracken became the official *picturer and drawer* to Lady Anne and in this role would have been exposed to a constellation of society's leading lights; his subjects included John Tufton, the second Earl of Thanet, royalist MP Sir Daniel Fleming, the Bishop of Carlisle Thomas Smith and King Charles I's wife, Queen Henrietta Maria. Although much is known about Lady Anne – her turbulent diaries are extant – not much more can be told of Bracken.

In 1979 Mary wrote *The Art of the Felt Maker*, recording the history of felt production, cataloguing important archaeological felt finds, discussing the mythology associated with felt and comparing feltmaking techniques around the world. The book was the first comprehensive history of felt. Works on Lake District artists William Green, Christopher Steele and Mathias Read followed in 1984 and 1986, the Green and Read books co-written with David Sloss, a retired Harley Street doctor who had settled in Bowness.

Londoner Read travelled with his master, Jan Wyck, to Whitehaven in West Cumbria around 1690, having been previously employed as painter to a naval sea captain of King William's fleet during the Battle of the Boyne. At the time of Read's arrival, Whitehaven was a boom town under the patronage of the coal and shipping Lowther magnates. Both Read and Jan Wyck were commissioned to paint for the family. Read's 1738 picture *A Bird's Eye View* dramatically shows John Lowther's plan of a well-laid-out affluent town. Read became very popular in Whitehaven. William Gilpin, agent to Sir John Lowther, wrote:

'There was hardly a house in Whitehaven whose master could afford it, which had not a picture or two painted on panels over doors or chimneys by his hand.'

In their book Mary and David Sloss describe how Read was one of the first native painters of the English landscape, a master of Cumbrian mountains and skies, a notable pre-picturesque painter of the Lake District. He spent the rest of his life in Whitehaven, teaching and painting, his portraits, landscapes and historical subjects adorning panels, doors and even ship's sterns.

On 8 November 1747 Read died aged 78 after a prolific working life. Five works by Read are recorded perished. Others stretch across the panels of Cumbrian homes, covered up with paint. Only fifty examples of his work survive catalogued. Among them is a pair depicting Mary's home, Isel Hall, both packed with detail. In the landscape painted from the north a mower lies under a tree, his blade pointing over his shoulder. A mounted horseman in a wide-brimmed black felt hat rides towards him. A horse plays with a dog and minute figures of cattle and horses appear in the middle distance. In the second of the pair, painted from the southern side of the River Derwent beside Setmurthy Forest, the little village of Blindcrake stands to the left of Isel.

'Two pairs of men talk in the lower left corner – the two on the extreme left are lolling on the rocks, and the two in blue and brown coats are possibly the owner (Sir Wilfred Lawson, 3rd Bt.) and a friend. One in each group is gesticulating as he talks.

'With masterly handling of the morning light Read has created one of his best skies. He uses the light to reveal the detail of the small escarpments in the otherwise dark foreground. This in itself anticipates the standardized late Georgian landscape "framing".'

In 1995 Mary tackled the fascinating story of George Smith, alias the Skiddaw Hermit, whose tale proper began in 1863 when he arrived in Keswick from a small place in Aberdeenshire called Pitsligo. Smith was a vagrant, a drinker, something of a mystic and a painter, born at Crossbrae in Banffshire in about 1825, one of eight children. His father was a crofter and ground officer on the estate of Sir Robert Abercromby.

'George attended Fordyce School and later Aberdeen University where, until his poor health forced him to give it up, he had a £16 bursary,' wrote Mary. 'His mother died when he was a child. His father married again but he too died shortly afterwards and the stepmother was very severe with George so that the day after his father's funeral he found himself homeless.'

Smith became a wanderer but although he lived roughly he was an attractive man. He had an eloquent voice, a lively expression of concentration and 'dove's eyes'. He acted like a gentleman and he kept himself clean.

'Soon after he came to the area, people noticed he went from Keswick every day to Skiddaw [a nearby mountain] and then returned to Keswick covered with mud each night. Eventually they discovered he had built himself a makeshift house on the slopes of the Dodd [a hill beside Skiddaw] on a ledge above a cave.' So began the legend of the Skiddaw Hermit (also alias The Dodd Man).

Smith had built a circular wall over which a dome-shaped roof of moss and bracken was suspended on wooden poles. He used old sacks or leaves for bedding and he lived alone, wary of visitors. He wore one shirt, washed in a nearby stream and dried on his back, and he walked barefoot. His trousers were cut off at the knees. He earned what he could by painting portraits or doing sketches of local people and possessed a passion for phrenology and physiognomy, feeling the bumps on people's heads at fairs, where he also preached sermons. His great love, however, was drink.

'It became a fashion for local innkeepers to have their portraits painted by him.' He could often be found in the Royal Oak, very drunk.

'Some of his habits were comic. He used to buy tea and sugar and eat them together, quite dry. When in funds he would buy steak, herring and potatoes and sometimes preferred to eat them raw, even the potatoes.'

Smith's intemperate behaviour eventually attracted the attention of the local police, who sent him up to Carlisle jail for non-payment of fines (where he painted the governor's portrait). On his return his shelter was wrecked by people he condemned as 'roisterous excursionists' and he moved from Keswick to Beech Hill near Ambleside, living in a small tent. When the drinking bouts started again he took up attacking passers-by. There was perhaps a brief recovery; it is said that he eventually stopped drinking and converted to Christianity, cutting the cover from a bible with a sharp knife and crying, 'This is to show you that henceforth this word of God must be an open book to me; it has been a closed book long enough.'

The conversion story may not be true. What is certain is that he returned to Scotland and died in a mental home in Banffshire in 1876.

In 1997 Mary collaborated with friend Valerie Rickerby to produce a biography of another Cumbrian artist, Percy Kelly. Both of them had known Kelly, who died in July 1993, at different times in his life. Valerie, a journalist, came across him when she reviewed his first exhibition at Whitehaven in December 1963. Mary met him via Robin Bagot, one of the Abbot Hall founders. In 1967 Kelly drew the black and white designs for the catalogue and invitation card to the 'One Thousand Years of Persian Art' exhibition and in 1976 Mary organised a major show of his work at Abbot Hall. Mary likens the partnership between herself and Valerie to that she shared with David Sloss – it was a pleasure dividing the load between two people passionate about their subject.

Percy Kelly was a superb artist who fell into deep depressions, an amateur footballer, a man plagued by damp walls and plumbing problems, a transvestite and the author of spectacular letters. Born Robert Percy Kelly on 3 November 1918, he grew up in a small terrace house on Corporation Road in Workington. His father was a master carpenter and his grandparents were strict Plymouth Brethren, a religion which counted among its prohibited activities swearing and playing football on Sundays. He excelled at art at the Central School for Boys in Salterbeck and showed great skill on the soccer field and cricket crease. At 14 he joined the Post Office as a telegraph boy.

'After a nine hour day from Monday to Saturday he went to the night school where, to his parents' amazement, he came second in the whole of the country in the Post and Telegraph Officers' entrance examinations and top in the country for handwriting.'

He quickly found a job at Workington and then Kendal Post Office, where he became a member of the Kendal Art Society. When he reluctantly returned to Workington he met and fell in love with Audrey James, who shared his delight in nature and walking. During the Second World War Kelly was posted to the 6th Battalion Border Regiment at Kendal, where he did a great deal of painting, thanks to the help of old friends in the Kendal Art Society.

'He also found time to help his fellow recruits, some of whom were illiterate, by drawing the different parts of the guns they used in training. This had a far greater impact on their understanding than written instructions.'

In 1940 he was transferred to the Royal Signals in Derby and later to the GHQ Home Forces section in London, working in a room next to Winston Churchill, whom he saw frequently but to whom it was strictly forbidden to speak.

In June 1944 Kelly crossed the channel in a Manx Steam Packet vessel for the D-Day landings, becoming bogged down on the outskirts of Bayeux and boiling water to bath small French children who were covered in sores. From there he followed the troops to Caen, Serquigny and finally Munster, setting up signal offices as he went. Thanks to the courtesy of some German telegraph workers he heard Churchill give the VE speech. During the entire conflict he had been painting and three of his watercolours were hung at a Forces' exhibition in the National Gallery.

'His chief hobby is art on which he spends the whole of his spare time,' wrote his senior officer as part of a glowing testimonial.

Kelly married Audrey James in 1942 during leave. In March 1946 he returned to civilian life, Audrey and his job in Workington, and in 1952 took over a small country Post Office at Great Broughton, near Cockermouth. Audrey did much of the office work to allow

Kelly time to go out into the countryside and to paint. In 1955 he was elected to the Lake Artists Society. Around this time he also joined Workington Football Club, under the management of Bill Shankly (who went on to achieve great fame and success as Liverpool manager). Newspaper cuttings record Kelly's 'sterling service' to the club. However, life at home was not so successful.

'Whether it was because he had to spend more time behind the Post Office counter because Audrey had a baby to look after, or whether it was increasing frustration with his artistic work, in 1958 he suffered a nervous breakdown. His doctor advised him to concentrate solely on his creative work and so he resigned his post at Great Broughton and in the autumn the family moved to Glen Cottage, Allonby, a small village on the Solway coast. With the help of yoga he nursed himself back to health and weaned himself off the drugs which had been prescribed to combat his illness.' A cycle of inspiration, followed swiftly by depression, had begun.

'The urge to become a full-time artist was gathering momentum and he applied in 1960 for the four-year course at Carlisle College of Art, only to be refused a grant on the grounds that he was too old. He was 42 at the time.'

Working as a night nurse for a year helped him pay for the course and eventually he won grant aid and a travelling scholarship to Brittany. Despite good reports from the college he was unable to find a teaching post when he graduated. Kelly, now 46, was saved from a deepening depression by Sir Nicholas Sekers, who commissioned him to complete a series of paintings of the interior of the Silk Mills at Hensingham, Whitehaven, which Sekers had founded. Exhibitions in Whitehaven followed but the strain of the artist's life told on his marriage. In 1970 he left Audrey and son Brian and went to live at Rosehill near Whitehaven in a flat provided by Sir Nicholas's son-in-law.

'He did not see his son again for the next twenty-four years when Brian visited him as he lay dying in hospital in Norwich.'

Kelly wasn't alone for long. In 1970 he began to have trouble with his eyes and sought help from a consultant called Paul Griffiths.

'By chance I was introduced to his wife and as time went by we fell in love,' wrote Kelly. He married Christine, who was also an artist, in 1971. They moved into a cottage at Levens owned by Robin Bagot. It was at this time that Mary met Kelly and their friendship began. (Mary would help him arrange exhibitions of his work and sent him money when he was broke.)

In 1973 Kelly and Christine moved to St David's in Wales, into two condemned cottages, numbers 5 and 7 Gospel Lane. The artist spent hours attending to the plumbing, electrics, plastering, building and joinery. It was a long struggle; he hunted out second-hand materials, grew vegetables in the garden and was bolstered by loans from benefactors like Kendal businessman Peter Scott. Two of Christine's three children, who had moved to Wales with them, slept in a tent around the back. There was a dispute over land with the neighbours. Eventually Kelly began to feel oppressed by the Pembrokeshire landscape, by the lack of progress on the house, the paucity of painting, which had suffered because of the building work, and by the weather. Depression returned.

In 1980, after the Gospel Lane work had finished, Kelly and Christine moved to St Peter near Attleborough in Norfolk. Although they made an £11,000 profit on the sale of the Welsh property, the Norfolk cottage was very small and needed an extra bedroom and kitchen. Despite this setback, the Kellys were very optimistic about their future in Norfolk. Christine's children, whose relationship with Kelly was 'rocky', had moved out. Christine told Kelly she had never been so happy and she began to fill the garden with sunflowers, honeysuckle and bedding plants. However, by the winter of 1982 seasonal gloom descended on the household. Kelly developed tinnitus and Christine had trouble with her sinuses.

Then in March 1983, without any warning, Christine left. Kelly was devastated by her departure. In November 1984 he wrote to Valerie Rickerby:

'When my wife disappeared one March day last year everything came to an end. I painted my last major picture in the summer of '82 and only the third since '76, so my output has been pathetic . . . My wife grew to hate the landscape and the people when we lived in Wales and, when we came here, after less than two years she began to hate Norfolk.'

The story behind Christine's 'disappearance' is not so simple. Before she left, Kelly had begun to wear women's clothes and call himself Roberta.

'In many people born with the gift of creative genius there is often a delicate balance between male and female genes,' wrote Mary and

Valerie. 'Most of Percy's friends were women so it was not surprising that in his distressed state he found consolation and companionship in becoming like them.'

The book does not record how long Kelly's transvestite period lasted, but its authors suggest it was public enough to provoke ridicule from his neighbours.

'There used to be five houses where I could call for a chat and cup of tea, now there are none, having been insulted and told not to return,' Kelly wrote. 'Even the shops I go to for the odd thing and baccy have turned hostile.'

On Christmas Day 1985 Kelly wrote that he suffered from periods of almost unbearable loneliness. His health began to deteriorate. In early 1993 a lump appeared in his throat. It was cancer. He was given chemotherapy and admitted to hospital but his condition declined rapidly. On 3 July he died. David Ralli, husband to Jacky (a former art student of Mary's), was with him at the very end.

'The only mention of death he made was about two hours before he died. "You know none of us can comprehend death – it is a far too complicated subject for the human brain." The end was blissfully tranquil and, as one would wish for any friend, his breathing just slowed up slightly and then at 1.24 in the morning of 3 July he stopped breathing. He looked so peaceful there with his beautiful grey hair falling beneath his maroon woolly hat. It was typical of Percy that, even in death, he achieved perfection.'

After Kelly's funeral his son Brian found hundreds of paintings at Pear Tree Cottage. The work ranged from delicate small paintings alive with colour and light to large black and white landscapes on a grander scale. Over the years he had produced not only watercolours and oils, but prints, etchings and lithographs.

'Percy Kelly has left an important collection of watercolours and drawings depicting all aspects of Cumbria,' wrote Valerie and Mary. 'His huge harbour scenes are masterful impressions of the maritime activity of Whitehaven, Workington and Maryport. His intimate view of tiny villages nestling in their hidden valleys show a timelessness of life in our area. His valley and hills of remoter places are strong, sensuous renderings of our time and weather-worn land. None of his work is sentimental or purely topographical. Although he loved detail, he never allowed this detail to spoil his bold artistic interpretation of nature.'

44. Richard Long

45. Stone Circle *by Richard Long*

46. Patrick Heron receiving an award

47. *Sheila Fell's* Scene near Aspatria

48. *Lucie Rie*

49. Lord Eccles and Sir Roger Fulford, Chairman of Trustees, opening an exhibition, with Mary.
Photograph courtesy of the Lancashire Evening Post

50. Dr David Bellamy

51. David Attenborough with Mary, opening the Qashqai Exhibition. Photograph courtesy of the Westmorland Gazette

52. Princess Alia of Jordan and entourage came to open the Jordanian Exhibition, Abbot Hall. Photograph courtesy of the Westmorland Gazette

53. Prince Charles with Mary and Patrick Gordon-Duff-Pennington at the opening of the County Council Environment Centre at Threlkeld

54. Princess Alexandra with Lord Lieutenant Paul Wilson, chairman of Lakeland Life and Industry Governors, and Mary, 1971

55. Princess Alexandra, Chancellor, Lancaster University, presenting Mary with an Hon. MA, 1997

56. Jenny Cowern with Sky Felt

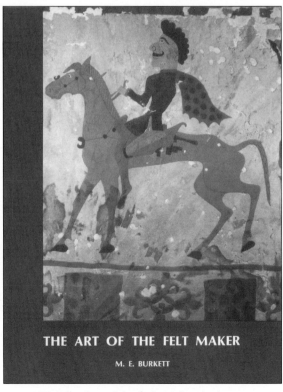

THE ART OF THE FELT MAKER

M. E. BURKETT

57. The Art of the Felt Maker book cover

58. Mary having received her OBE in 1978

59. Carel Waite, Portrait of Mary. *Photograph courtesy of the* Westmorland Gazette

60. The William Green Exhibition at Dove Cottage

61. Edith Thomas *by Kurt Schwitters*

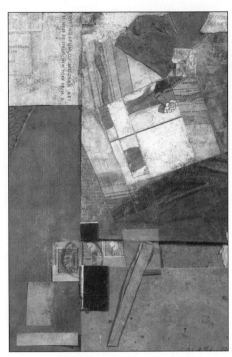

62. Collage detail YMCA Flag, Ambleside
by Kurt Schwitters, at Abbot Hall

63. Lady Anne Clifford, aged 15

64. May Moore on book cover

65. HM The Queen's visit to Abbot Hall in 1986

66. Margaret Austen-Leigh

67. *Mary in an amusement park in Hong Kong*

68. Felt coat *by Beth Beede*

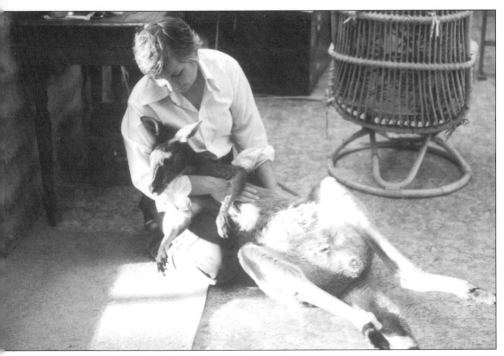

69. *Mary stayed with Theresa Lawrence and her tame kangaroo, Blossom while in Australia*

70. Isel Hall, south façade

71. Isel Hall, north façade and pele tower

72. *Mathias Read's* Bird's Eye View of Whitehaven

73. *Alfred Wainwright's pen and ink drawing of Mary's house Demavend*

74. Taj Mahal

75. Svetlana Alliluyeva, Stalin's daughter, taken by her daughter Olga

There is a striking austerity in the work of Percy Kelly. His landscapes are empty of humans and animals, and as a result we are drawn closer to the buildings, the houses, the fields and the skies. There are no distractions. His etchings, in particular, capture the hard edges, flat light, dark skies and lonely roads of Cumbria. His art spilled over into his correspondence: his remarkable letters include beautiful calligraphy and are headed with fascinating drawings of old ships or cars, engines, buildings, landscapes. A selection fills the final pages of Mary and Valerie's book. Above the immaculate hand-writing stretch watercolour sketches of Cockermouth and Maryport, a dinner table laden with food and wine (bought with birthday money sent by Mary), a Morris Minor traveller, a rock pool, armchairs, cottages, sailing ships, a farm near Fishguard on a horrible damp New Year's Day. The text sometimes spills into the paintings, sometimes crawls around them or folds into a floor, a road, a hillside. Even Percy Kelly's envelopes are ornate, bearing trawler boats, steamships and majestic swans.

I Was Only A Maid, published in 1998, was something of a departure for Mary, being a biography of May Moore, fashioned from Mary's interviews with May, her family and friends. May was a former maid at Isel Hall, the stately home Mary inherited in 1986, and she had spent much of her life in service. She had also worked as Beatrix Potter's hairdresser, seamstress and helper and she was something of a 'free spirit' – she was 68 when she first tried hang gliding.

May was born on 7 May 1907, her father Thomas a chauffeur to Sir Wilfred Lawson, owner of Isel Hall. As May travelled to Isel church to be christened alongside her twin brother, Lady Lawson came out onto the terrace of Isel Hall and said to Thomas, 'Moore, I want the boy to be called Derwent, born on the River Derwent and the girl to be called May, born in the month of May.' He agreed. The gentry, it seemed, were Adamic in their power.

In November 1918 Thomas died, a victim of the flu epidemic at 57 years old. May and her younger brother Arthur were told by their mother that their father had passed away and was 'down in the churchyard'. Unsure exactly what this meant, they collected a spade and a fork, put a candle in a jamjar and set out in the dark from Bloomire Cottage, intent on disinterring their unfortunate father. Thankfully their mother intercepted them and the scheme was abandoned.

Like Mary, May was a spirited woman, as she too demonstrated at an early age. As a twelve-year-old schoolgirl she refused to curtsy to the headmaster and was immediately called out to the front of the class, to be given four strokes of the cane. On the second stroke she fainted, was carried outside and laid on the road beside a stream. When she came to, May tumbled into the water and cracked her head on a rock. She was found by a certain Harry Sandwith, who tied her to him and took her on a horse to Cockermouth Cottage Hospital, where she spent three days with a bandaged head.

At thirteen, May left school and went to work as an under parlour-maid in the Lawson household. Duties included waiting at table, ironing newspapers, cleaning fireplaces and tidying rooms, for which she was paid £1.15 a month. It was gruelling work but there were occasional treats – such as a trip to Blackpool in a charabanc with hard pneumatic tyres or a ride over Isel in a bi-plane piloted by the aeronaut Sir Wilfred, May's black mourning ribbon streaming out from under a flying helmet. On shooting days she would serve the beaters 'Tatie Ash' and plum pudding in the racquet courts. When the hunt was riding she presented the men with their stirrup cups and the ladies with violets.

Aged twenty, after being promoted to parlour-maid, May left Isel to work at nearby Higham for six years and from Higham she moved to Hampshire to be the lady's maid to the wife of Sir Alexander Gibb. In 1936, homesick, she turned north again to take a position as head housemaid for the mother of a Major Hext in Hollyworth, near Coniston, cycling thirty-nine miles every month to visit her sick mother. It was at Coniston that May met Mrs Heelis, also known as Beatrix Potter. One day there was a knock at the door, heralding a plump lady in a shabby tweed suit who promptly asked May if she cut hair.

'Yes I do,' May replied, spreading a sheet across the dining room floor as Mrs Heelis sat down impatiently. When Mrs Hext arrived she was somewhat taken aback to find Mrs Heelis's long locks being reduced to a bob in her dining room. When May had finished Mrs Heelis said cryptically, 'I'll take the hair. I have a use for it.'

Over the next few years May – christened 'The Little One' by Heelis – went on to help the eccentric author with her darning, sewing and washing. She was later engaged to clean Hilltop, Heelis's house, washing the flag floor and removing cobwebs alongside two other maids while Heelis sat at her easel on her old chair.

At the age of forty-three May ended her life of service, taking a job at a clothing factory in Cockermouth to support her ailing mother. She worked there for seventeen years before retiring. In 1975 she decided to travel to New Zealand to visit an old school friend – where she tried hang gliding and loved it. In retirement May returned to the place of her first appointment, giving talks about her work at Isel to visiting tourists and replying in the same way when (very rarely) she did not know the answer to a visitor's question, 'I was only a maid.'

On 1 June 1986 Mary retired from Abbot Hall in a flurry of farewell parties. She was determined to be as active as ever. With customary zest she applied for a Leverhulme Fellowship to catalogue portraits in Cumbria, a project she had started at Abbot Hall. Together with her friend Leslie Randall, who photographed each painting in turn for the survey, she made a record of over 3,000 pictures in more than a hundred houses, castles and stately homes. Sometimes she would travel outside Cumbria to Lancashire, Dumfries and even the Isle of Man, to track portraits which had passed over the county-line.

Mary's contacts from Kendal helped, and again she benefited from the generosity of spirit which characterised the friends and patrons of Abbot Hall. When Mary asked to view a painting in a house whose occupants were absent, keys were left with staff and plates of food sat beside messages of goodwill in country kitchens. People liked the attention their pictures received.

For a woman who nurtured childhood dreams of being a detective, the scholarship was a gift to early aspirations. New portraits by Lakeland masters were uncovered in dusty corners of remote farmhouses, new mysteries hung in town parlours, paintings whose subjects were forgotten ancestors, whose provenance was unknown, whose artists were disputed. Like the daily grind of a private detective, much of Mary's work was confidential; her records were kept in code in order to baffle potential thieves.

When Mary retired from Abbot Hall the Friends commissioned artist Carel Waite to paint her portrait and raised £5,000 to fund a round-the-world trip. Mary was delighted and she began preparing for an adventure that would take her to India, China, Hong Kong, New Zealand, Australia and America. In the middle of her planning

Mary learnt that Margaret Austen-Leigh, a friend and distant relative, had died. Mary was to inherit Mrs Austen-Leigh's home of Isel Hall, a grand stately house complete with pele tower and magnificent gardens, standing above the River Derwent near Cockermouth in Cumbria. She set off on her tour dazed by this incredible and unexpected news.

From the grey fug of smoggy Delhi, where sacred cows stood like islands in a sea of cyclists, rickshaw drivers rattled along the streets and three-wheeled motorbikes carried a muddle of passengers under coloured canopies, Mary's party took a coach to Agra. Oxen with painted hides bellowed in the fields and scarlet saris fluttered from the pillion seats of a sea of scooters.

'A forlorn camel dragged a cart as the road narrowed and became a single track,' Mary wrote in her diary. 'Barbers shaved customers in the street, a woman balanced two big pots on her head, one above the other. Children made patty cakes of dung for fuel, leaving them in prettily arranged patterns to dry in the sun.'

The bus bumped past little thatched mud huts standing in bamboo thickets, hazy paths that stretched into the horizon and rivers where black kingfishers hunted, finally rattling into Agra and beyond to the Taj Mahal, the great dome glistening with jasper, cornelian and agate, reminding Mary of the blue mosque in faraway Isfahan.

Flying to Hong Kong through tiny white cumulus cloud, Mary saw Calcutta and the Bay of Bengal slip away beneath her, the Ganges drain to the sea and the white peaks of Tibet shimmer in the distance. The city state, with its stalagmitic mass of skyscrapers, felt like a different century after Delhi.

'The weather turned rotten and it poured, but no matter. All the Chinese umbrellas came out in the phantasmagoria of floral patterns, checks and columns.'

Hong Kong was little more than a whistle stop and soon Mary was standing before the Ming Temple of Heaven in Beijing, a fifteenth-century masterpiece of Chinese architecture.

'It was a hazy morning, with the pale pinky sun struggling behind thin smoke, grey houses behind our six-lane route with cycle tracks on one side. It was reminiscent of an empty, spacious Moscow.'

The temple was a blossom of bright pagodas, ornamental watch-towers, delicate carving and crafted stone. Bamboo surrounded the building, and a nearby panda house held a single unfortunate creature in a dull concrete room, a bundle of bamboo shoots in one corner. Nearby stood the Summer Palace, 280 hectares of parks and residencies for the emperor's household, built in 1888, complete with a marble boat. Locust trees, crab apples and cypress surrounded the adjoining Temple of the Thousand Buddhas. Light sparkled from across a nearby lake onto the pagodas and tiny Chinese children wrapped in voluminous woollen coats toured the temple, their faces crinkling easily to laughter.

At Badaling near the Great Wall (a dragon's back riding the hills from the Gobi to the sea) a peasant in black jacket, dull grey trousers and a pale faded mauve cap dragged a pile of faggots behind him. The sun-washed blue doors of his red brick village were hidden behind a maze of trees, their leaves fluttering in the breeze. Creamy white goats grappled with yellow maize stalks and a tiny black piglet ran along a path littered with leaves. From the wall Mary surveyed the green hills beyond, silent history beneath her feet.

Beijing was surrounded by snow when she left for Xi'an, home of the terracotta warriors that guard the tomb of the Emperor Qin Shi Huang. Here eight thousand silent soldiers – infantrymen, archers, crossbow carriers, and cavalrymen – fill three underground halls. They stand in battle formation around the emperor's tomb, some stepping forward in attack and others kneeling with swords drawn, ready to withstand the invader. Their horses carry bronze bridles, and to Mary's delight, the archers are depicted wearing felt tunics.

At Shanghai Mary found a throbbing, thriving city. Washing fluttered over narrow streets like colossal bunting, hung with the help of long bamboo ladders. Shanghai's colonial past was evident in French architecture and Japanese pillboxes. The tourist authorities were keener on showing Mary's party a city commune than the exotic underside of Shanghai, and they were lectured on the efficiency of commune hospital, dentist and farm. A tour around the Chinese premier's residency followed, during which their guide became suddenly agitated, ushering the group back to their car.

'I looked around to see why. There, walking up towards us, surrounded by twelve security men, was a little old man in a black cap.' Deng Xiaoping, leader of China, was taking a walk. He bowed respectfully to the tourists and left them huddled in amazement.

Mary spent Christmas and New Year in Perth, Australia, as the house guest of friends James Trevelyan, an engineer and inventor, and his wife Jo. After a morning watching honeyeaters zip across the gardens she would drive out to the Pinnacles (mineral pillars that gathered around the roots of ancient trees and now stand like modern sculptures), watch the races at Freemantle or spend an afternoon on the beach. She sketched deserted beaches around Perth, scrub bush, blowholes and turquoise seas. In the Aboriginal museum she was drawn to pictures of tribal markings, strip wounds into which sand was rubbed before they were left to close and scar forever. ABC radio interviewed her about felt and at Bunbury, home to an Australian feltmaking group, she was given a hearty welcome.

In the new year, Mary set off for New Zealand, where she stayed with the former Ambleside student Jocelyn Davison and her husband David, at their sheep farm at Lowry Peaks in North Canterbury. In the Weka Pass she stood amazed before the Maori paintings, where strange men with three-pronged weapons shared a craggy limestone canvas with long lizards and blunt-nosed sharks. Jocular dinners followed flights in David's plane, the pilot clinging close to jagged spurs below, mountains at each side, finally bumping across into the valley of Lake Summer.

Next stop Fiji, the Sky Lodge resort and Mala Mala (Day Dream) island, set 'under a brilliant blue sky in a brilliant blue sea, covered in white sand and mango trees. There was a real party atmosphere – they had us all dancing on the boat over . . . quite ridiculous.' She spent the day as castaway, collecting shells, eating mangoes and listening to the gentle lisp of the sea.

The trip was nearing its end. In San Francisco she stayed with David Stronach, her old friend from the Gunbad-i-Qabus dig and Professor of Middle Eastern Architecture at Berkeley University, his house a trove of Qajar paintings, Persian and Turcoman rugs and a menagerie for cats. Mary wandered the streets of San Francisco and attended archaeological lectures. She sat up late at night talking about Iran with David and friends, bemoaning arms deals and corruption, religious intolerance and the bombing of beautiful Isfahan.

It was wintertime and it grew colder as she travelled east to Northampton in Massachusetts to visit artist and feltmaker Beth Beede. The house was humming with delegates of a felt conference that Beth had organised and Mary slept on the floor surrounded by felt carpets. Further east in Long Island she met Roy Nicholson, the former arts officer for Cumbria who now teaches in America, and recalls standing on the beach near his house, watching the water gradually freeze, icicles gathering on the pier, as grebes and gulls made slow progress across the sky. There was just enough time to visit friends in Richmond, Virginia, before it was time to go home. It had been a magical trip but Isel beckoned.

CHAPTER 7

Isel

A METAL SIGN POINTS TO ISEL from the Cockermouth road, Skiddaw skulking in the distance, its broad shoulders stretching east. Down in the valley the muddy River Derwent slowly sweeps under a stone bridge. Cross the wide water, turn left, past the old vicarage and a little Norman church, and Isel Hall looms into view. At first sight it is daunting, standing on a steep rise over the river, the pele tower and the wide west-facing walls giving it an air of fortitude and defiance. As part of a chain of Border forts the tower and Great Hall were built on the site of a much older structure, severely damaged when the Scots raided Cockermouth in 1387. Isel is a legacy of the reivers, family bands of cattle rustlers and raiders, when the border between England and Scotland was a grey area of attack and counterattack, of raids and cattle rustling, of summary justice and defence in stone.

The Hall was built on the north side of the river because at that time the land there was thickly forested to prevent attack from Normans and later Scots. Traces of a moat are evident on the north and east side of the tower, itself the bolthole of early owners; if Scots troops were spotted in the distance, the owners would gather their family and most treasured possessions, climb up to the tower by an open wooden stair on the south side of the building, then kick away the stairs, lock the door, piling furniture against it for good measure, then pray that trouble passed them by. During Tudor times, when the border was hotly disputed and the machinations of both English and Scots courts encouraged a wild and wanton rule of law, the threat was greatest. It was only with the ascension of James I, King of both Scotland and England, that the reivers' stronghold on Cumberland was wrestled away by firmer government.

The origin of Isel's name is as murky as the Derwent in spate. In the ancient official documents called Pipe Rolls, the place was called *Ysala*, meaning Isa's river meadow but *Isel* is also the Welsh for low and could refer to the valley setting. Whatever the provenance, it was not permanent – the name changed from *Ysala* to *Yshale, Ishale, Isale,*

Issell, *Isell* and finally, from 1850 onwards *Isel*. When William Rufus reoccupied Cumberland at the end of the eleventh century Ysala was granted to Ranulph Engayne. In 1138 Ranulph's granddaughter and heiress Ada married Simon de Morville, lord of the barony of Burgh. Their son, Hugh, eventually took possession.

Local legend had it that Isel was here ushered in to play a small and shameful part in the story of the English throne – this Sir Hugh Morville was one of the four knights who murdered Thomas Becket, Archbishop of Canterbury, on 29 December 1170 – but that tale is no longer given much credence by historians. This Hugh Morville's sword, listed among Isel's inventory in 1706 but lost in a fire in Brayton Hall (an Aspatria manor-house that came into the Lawson family at the end of the seventeenth century), is unlikely to be the same one that kept gathering clerics at bay while Reginald Fitzurse, William de Tracey, Richard le Breton brained Becket.

Sir Hugh's mother, Ada, was a similarly controversial figure locally. Several histories describe how she lusted after a servant of her husband called Lyolfe Young. Loyal to his master, Lyolfe refused her advances, only to warm her passion further. Delivering a dish of meat to her bedroom, he found the door locked behind him. Ada begged him to sleep with her and when he refused once more, her hunger bubbled into anger. She screamed (unlocked the door) and when her husband burst into the room, accused the poor Lyolfe of attempted rape. The young servant was promptly bound and cast into a cauldron of boiling water. It must have been an excruciatingly painful death but perhaps one that has been avenged; a pale lady in a blue dress haunts Isel. Her features are opaque and indeterminate. She appears to male guests only and three men who have slept in the small bedroom on the main wing of Isel during Mary's tenure have seen her floating towards them during the night. On one occasion Liam McDowall, a teenage friend of Mary's, watched in horror as she slipped around the bed and climbed onto his chest. It seems the ghost of Ada is trapped in a sexual purgatory, condemned to press her advances onto yet more unwilling men.

After Sir Hugh's death another Ada Morville, the elder of his two daughters, took possession of Isel. She married Richard de Lucy of Egremont in 1204 but the de Lucy family had a fleeting grasp of Isel. Richard left no male heir and when he died his widow Ada married Thomas de Multon.

By the chance of succession and inheritance, Isel had fallen into the hands of the Leigh family by the reign of Edward II, who took the throne in 1307. The Leighs were to hold on to the manor for 250 years and it was a Leigh who rebuilt Isel after the Earls of Douglas and Fife raided Cockermouth in 1387 and destroyed the original buildings. One of the family's most illustrious sons was Robert Leigh, who owned lands in Norfolk as well as Cumberland. Robert was over fifty when he inherited Isel in 1494 and a man of great wealth and influence. He also played a part in a bizarre trial at Hexham, assisting in the prosecution concerning the murder of his relative Alexander Dykes. The entire trial was a family affair; the case had been brought by Dykes's widow Elizabeth and the accused were Sir Thomas Curwen and his son Christopher, relatives of Leigh and Dykes. The Curwens were found guilty but because their victim had been kin, their bizarre penalty was to 'show themselves meekly sorry for the death' of Alexander, and to pay Elizabeth £80 in two instalments, £40 on the feast of St Michael the Archangel and the other £40 at the feast of St Peter. They were also ordered to find a priest to sing for the soul of Dykes in the church at Isel.

By the time Henry VIII was making an enemy of the Pope, John Leigh had inherited Isel. Once again, the estate was given a walk-on part in England's play. Henry had ordered the dissolution of the monasteries, demanding that they be torn down and sacked. One of the men to do his bidding was Dr Thomas Leigh, younger brother of Sir John, who secured the surrender of Holme Cultram Abbey, fifteen miles north of Isel. The Leighs were well paid for their part in this ecclesiastical terrorism – the lands and assets of Holme Cultram simply passed to the family and Sir John became its Steward.

Both brothers entered directly into the service of the King and family fortunes continued to soar. By November 1538 John was living in a very spacious house in Venice. He visited Rome in December and returned to Isel in 1539. He became High Sheriff of Cumberland and Westmorland in 1547/8 and died in 1563. Dr Thomas inherited the estates and gave Isel to his second wife Maud Redmain, who afterwards married the Yorkshireman William Lawson. The Leigh reign at Isel was over; the Lawsons' sun had definitely risen. Their coat of arms (the hands of law holding a smiling sun) became Isel's. Wilfred was given a knighthood by James I, leaving a line of descendants and Isel owners who shone in the courts of subsequent kings.

When Joseph Pennell came across Isel in the 1730s, at the head of the Isel household sat Wilfred, a groom of the bedchamber to King George I and, like his father before him, MP for Cockermouth. Pennell, writing in his *Highways and Byways of the Lake District*, recalls the sad story of Wilfred's eldest daughter Elizabeth, a maid to the King's daughter, Princess Charlotte, and infamous loser in love. Her paramour was Major James Wolfe, who would one day become the posthumous hero of the English war against France in Quebec. At 21 he was already a veteran of six years' service in the wars against the French. Elizabeth was a beautiful favourite at court. They met in London. Pennell wrote:

'Wolfe formed an attachment to the lady of so ardent a nature as to prove destructive to his peace of mind for an unconscionably long period.'

Unfortunately for Elizabeth, Wolfe may have been a war hero but he was also a mummy's boy; his mother was determined he marry a rich heiress from a family of greater social standing than Elizabeth's and she said such horrible things about the maid that Wolfe had his first and only quarrel with his mother. The fight so upset the devoted son that he ran away to Scotland to take up garrison duty. He also cut off all communication with Elizabeth. They never saw each other again but, wrote Pennell, for many years mere sight of Elizabeth's picture on the wall 'took away Wolfe's appetite for dinner'. They both died unmarried.

A bewildering assortment of Wilfred Lawsons followed, including The Clogs Baronet. An elected Knight of the Shire of Cumberland, he carried a loaf of barley bread and a pair of clogs into the House of Commons in 1760 as visual aids to his campaign against land tax.

The Wilfred Lawson of 1829–1906 displayed similar reforming zeal. An orator, poet, huntsman and temperance fan, he bought John Peel's hunting pack after Peel's death and became master of the Cumberland Foxhounds. He was also a frequent supporter of unpopular causes, tabling a Bill for the suppression of alcohol and taking presidency of the UK Alliance for Prohibition. He defended women's rights in 1869, was an advocate of religious equality (supporting the atheist Bradlaugh when he was excluded from Parliament), Irish Nationalism and the Boers. He was one of only two

MPs who backed Sir Charles Dilke's motion to investigate the expenditure of the revered Queen Victoria. Despite his reputation as a firebrand, his legendary good humour meant he was short of enemies.

In 1869 this Wilfred married Mary Pocklington-Senhouse, daughter of Joseph Pocklington and Elizabeth Senhouse. A scrap of paper found in a drawer of a table in Isel's dining room records the story of Jane Campbell, who married the roguish Roger Pocklington in 1802. The newlyweds rode back from the ceremony to their house on the same horse and crossing a river, Jane fell off. Reaching home Roger asked a servant to unhorse Mrs Pocklington. On being told she was not there he simply said:

'I thought I heard a little splash.'

The story of Isel's owners approaches its end, but not before the reappearance of the Leigh family. In 1960 Margaret Austen-Leigh, great-great-granddaughter of the wet Mrs Pocklington, reclaimed the estate when it had to be sold. (Her husband Richard a publisher, printer and writer who revised the edited works of his great-aunt Jane Austen, died just one year after coming to Isel, leaving his wife to breed Shetland ponies and large poodles in the grounds.) Margaret Austen-Leigh died childless in 1986 and Isel came to Mary Burkett, her friend and distant relative. Mrs Austen-Leigh and Mary's maternal grandfather, James Gaussen of Armagh, were both descendants of former Isel owners, the Sotheby family. This connection, made when Sarah Sotheby married the Reverend Armytage Gaussen in 1792, is the pivot on which this book turns. It is the reason that when I discovered Isel, driving up the gravel track on a sunny afternoon to take a closer look at the remarkable building, I also discovered Mary Burkett.

Today the raiders who can be spotted dashing towards Isel from the top of the pele tower are not border bandits, but tourists greeted warmly; on one afternoon every week in the summer the Hall is open for visitors, and guides are on hand to show people through the impressive hallway, the secretive Oak Room, the imposing tower and the Elizabethan bedrooms. Other visitors arrive unexpectedly, like Svetlana Alliluyeva, better known as the only daughter of Joseph Stalin.

'Some friends [the Kellys of Lorton Hall] rang up and asked if they could bring her to tea at Isel,' Mary nonchalantly recalls. (Lawrence Kelly was, like Svetlana, descended from Georgian stock.)

Mary's main worry was not how should she react when meeting the only daughter of the twentieth century's most ruthless mass murderer, but whether there was enough cake to go round. She rushed out to buy an orange iced sponge and some chocolate biscuits, cutting up cucumber sandwiches in a rush before the guests arrived.

'I made a bit of a fuss of her when she came to the door with these two friends. I welcomed her . . . just politely. She came in and I asked her if she would like tea on the terrace or in the dining room. "Out on the terrace," she said, sweeping past.

'We sat taking in the view, she looking absolutely amazed at this lovely summer day, the river flowing along, green and pleasant. She was oohing and aahing. We talked. She wouldn't touch any cake.'

Before she left, a chord had been struck and a friendship forged. Svetlana asked Mary if she could come and work as a cook at Isel. She had been captivated by the place.

'We just formed this immediate friendship. I liked her. I wasn't putting it on. She was very strong, her cheekbones were a bit like her father's and she was about my age. She loves cooking and she reads a lot and I thoroughly enjoyed reading the manuscripts she was intending to publish. She's a very lively person with a lively mind. She does find it quite difficult to make friends.'

Soon the pair began writing letters to each other, starting a regular course of correspondence that has lasted for years. In that time Mary was to learn some of the darkest secrets of Stalin's daughter.

Svetlana Alliluyeva is the daughter of Stalin's second wife, Nadezhda Alliluyeva. Stalin's first wife Ekaterina Svanidze had died in 1907 of tuberculosis and their son Yasha perished in a Nazi prison camp. In 1919 Stalin married Nadezhda (also called Nadya) and Svetlana was born in 1926.

Her father's home life as a child had been miserable – her grandfather Vissarion Dzhugashvili was a poor drunken shoemaker who beat young Joseph savagely – and Svetlana's childhood was scarred by her own parents' bitter quarrels. On one occasion Nadya took Svetlana and her older brother Vasily to live with her family in Leningrad, 'forever'. She returned, though, and a type of peace returned, although Stalin resented Nadya's attempts to interfere with party business. As Stalin's powers increased, Nadya grew jealous. Women openly flirted with her husband and Stalin enjoyed the attention.

'Mama thought more and more frequently of leaving my father,' wrote Svetlana later. Stalin began to respond to his admirers, betraying Nadya with increasing frequency. Then on 8 November 1932 tragedy struck. At an anniversary party Nadya and Stalin argued – he had been flirting with a colleague's wife. Nadya left the party in a dark mood, went home and bolted her door. She apparently wrote a letter, which has disappeared, and shot herself in the heart with a little Walther revolver, the rose she had worn in her hair to attract Stalin's wandering eye falling to the floor beside her bleeding body. Stalin immediately made her suicide a state secret and the truth was hidden from everyone, including Svetlana.

Stalin was, of course, one of the most ruthless dictators of modern times, accused of wanton slaughter during the pre-war political trials of former comrades, of causing thousands of unnecessary casualties and deaths during the Second World War by interfering with Red Army campaigns, of ordering the murder of thousands of Polish prisoners of war and of tyrannical despotism on a grand scale. But it was the fact that he, in effect, killed her mother that Svetlana finds most hard to bear, says Mary.

'It is human nature that rules the world, not governments and regimes,' Svetlana once wrote in the *New York Times*.

After her mother's death Svetlana was promoted to the title of 'lady of the house'. She adored her doting father. 'I shall never forget his affection, his love and tenderness to me as a child. I loved him tenderly, as he loved me,' she wrote.

To modern historians, after Nadya's death, Svetlana appears as the one human being to whom Stalin reached out. As he plotted the murder of his closest allies in a battle for power, he appeared to her as a loving father. It was only when someone gave her a British magazine to read in the winter of 1941 that she slowly discovered the truth about her family. Her mother's suicide was mentioned in the article. She was stunned.

'She told me of the long tortuous relationship that she had with him, realising more and more who he was and how he had effectively killed off her adored mother,' recounts Mary.

Svetlana's relationship with her father quickly cooled. When she fell in love with the writer Alexei Kapler and her father discovered she had a sweetheart, Kapler was arrested, denounced as a spy and banished to a forced labour camp for five years. Stalin slapped

Svetlana and said, 'Just look at yourself. Who do you think would want you? He's got women all over the place. You fool!' She stopped talking to him for several months. They became strangers. In 1944 Svetlana married a Jewish Moscow University student named Grigori Morozov. 'Do what the hell you like' was Stalin's reaction to the marriage. She gave birth to a boy, named after his grandfather, and shortly afterwards divorced Morozov. She then married Yuri Zhadanov but they parted in 1952.

On 5 March 1953 Svetlana was summoned to Stalin's dacha. Her father had suffered a stroke and was writhing on the floor.

'Father's death was slow and difficult . . . His face was discoloured and different . . . his features were becoming unrecognisable . . . The death agony was terrible. It choked him slowly as we watched. At the last minute he opened his eyes. It was a terrible look – either mad or angry and full of the fear of death . . . Suddenly he released his left hand and seemed either to be pointing upwards somewhere or threatening us all . . . then, the next moment, his spirit after one last effort tore itself from his body.'

She carried on her work as a teacher after Stalin's death but in 1966, while in India, defected to the West, settling in the United States in April 1967, leaving her son and daughter in the Soviet Union. She published her memoirs, *Twenty Letters to a Friend*, and in 1970 wed American architect William Peters, with whom she had a daughter. This third marriage was, again, soon over and Svetlana returned to the Soviet Union to live in Tiblisi, but her peregrinations were not over yet. In 1986 she again left the USSR and returned to the States, before moving to England; it was during this time that she met Mary and offered to be her cook. Mary declined.

'I didn't think it really would have worked, because I'm quite independent. It would have been wonderful to have been cooked for but she would never have found the right ingredients in my wretched kitchen,' says Mary. 'It was decided that she was going to go and live in Cornwall anyway.'

It was a short-lived stay – a Sunday paper blew her cover and her incognito existence was over – and she decided to return to America and her daughter.

'I thought – should I keep the friendship by letter only?' says Mary. 'No, she was lonely and she had had some horrid experiences in Britain, really horrid experiences. People chasing after her, being beastly to her, treating her like a foreigner and being rude to her. I went down to St Ives and we had a very pleasant weekend. We went out onto the peninsula that sticks out from St Ives and had a fantastic time just talking and sitting in the sun.' Svetlana gave her a silver brooch and Kashmir shawl as tokens of remembrance.

They still write to each other, Mary and her nearly-cook.

'I was afraid to open your letter when I collected it from my PO Box – I waited several hours to gather courage – for I was afraid that My Warrior is *sending me to Hell*,' writes the emotional Svetlana, explaining her fears that Mary, her warrior, wasn't interested in keeping the friendship alive. 'But when I, finally, read it – I was overjoyed. You are still my dearest Mary. I love you.

'I am always glad to hear about My Warrior's activities – whether a lecture or Felt exhibition, or just a [*sic*] travel to faraway Falklands . . . I'm sure that you always meet people who respond to your words and deeds – and isn't LIFE ALL about that?

'I always *loved* Friends, much more than *blood-relatives*, parents, even – yes – more than children! and *only in that* I could find real satisfaction and solace.'

She explains how she is often unhappy with her life, unsure of her daughter's plans, whom she lives with, and still restless. 'Your letters are so helpful here.'

Mary's adventures at Isel continue. When she is not watching birds or hunting Roman Roads, she battles to keep the weather from invading her beloved pele tower. She has employed the architect Michael Bottomley and builder Norman Tiffen to work on the restoration of the roof and the stonework, and surveyed several Cumbrian pele towers when deciding whether to render her own or leave the stones exposed to the elements. The Dowager Lady Egremont, resident at nearby Cockermouth Castle in the summer months, has known Mary since the late sixties. She says: 'I was impressed by her resilience and courage in taking over Isel. It was run down and it needed a lot of work. She moved in and straightaway made a go of it. She's not a tremendously domesticated person. But she has the feel of the place. It seems to be part of her, and she is part of it.'

'Despite many architectural changes Isel Hall has stood for nearly 1,000 years on the same spot,' writes Mary in her introduction to Valerie Rickerby's history of Isel (from which much of this chapter is drawn). 'Less dramatic but equally important are the minor daily demands of the fabric of the house. It leaks, it creaks, it almost breathes but despite these idiosyncrasies, which claim constant attention, it is calm, enveloping and protective and has acquired its own unique atmosphere.'

A house as old as Isel requires ingenuity in battling the elements. When writer David Cross first met Mary in 1989 he was most amazed by a Heath Robinson device she had created to encourage rainwater to run down a series of sticks placed beside the chimney in the old servants' hall, so it would collect in a bucket and not in the grate.

Cross, who moved to Isel in 1990, is one of several artists whom Mary has invited to live in the wings or converted stables there. He shared the west wing with Finbar O'Suilleabhain (a scholar researching the work of the composer Stockhausen) who would leave one or two of his roll-up cigarettes on the stairs each night for Mary to smoke. She retired with them to her cosy Oak Room, holding each between the blades of old scissors (to avoid nicotine stains) while sipping martini bianco or pink champagne.

Among her regular visitors Mary counts Liam McDowall, a United Nations official whom she first met as a little boy in the mid 1970s, in a 'mineral' shop in Bowness run by his mother and step-father. 'There were three little boys sitting on the floor,' recalls Mary, 'and they all had uncommonly bright, intelligent eyes. When I asked whose they were, the mother behind the counter said: "Mine and you can have that one [meaning Liam] – he's rude and disobedient." Or something to that effect. A few days later he began visiting me. At first we talked about stamps. I could hardly understand his broad Cumbrian accent but gradually we talked about anything, a lot of politics, as he was an ardent Communist in his early teens, and eventually art. "All modern art is roobish!" he used to say. All that changed . . . He took a degree in modern art from Newcastle.'

Isel can sometimes feel like an artists' colony. Cross recalls an impromptu concert given by a young Japanese violinist amid the sculptures of Josefina de Vasconcellos, a former Isel tenant. Another member of Isel's creative family was the potter Edward Hughes, who lived in the stables with his wife Shizuko and fired his work in the kiln beside Isel's squash court before his death in a tragic accident on Pillar Mountain in the spring of 2006.

If Isel is an artists' colony, it's a working colony. Both Cross and O'Suilleabhain were inveigled into helping Mary with domestic arrangements in return for reduced rent – O'Suilleabhain mowing Isel's lawns and feeding the geese, Cross weeding, planting, painting and pruning in the garden.

'Woe betide any gardener, visitor or tenant who mislaid garden tools,' writes Cross. 'Indeed, Mary could certainly be irascible when needed. This has doubtless been part of her successful repertoire of management skills. From time to time both manual workers and professionals felt the force of her wrath when events had not unfolded according to plan or any situation was deemed to be unacceptable . . . Occasionally she would apologise when she knew she had gone too far. When things went well, she was often generous with her praise and would sometimes offer tokens of appreciation.'

If you drive out from Cockermouth along the old Isel road, drop down into the valley, cross the bridge, and turn the corner you will spot the 'good house and a pleasant seat upon the bank of the River Derwent'. Isel may be open for visitors and your wheels crunch along the gravel driveway as you pass the sunken garden and approach the imposing pele tower, the geese honking a welcome. At the doorway or on the terrace there may be standing a woman with a thick mane of grey hair, her high cheekbones more prominent for a wide smile, her hands digging deep into the pockets of an old woollen cardigan as she leans forward, back straight. Shake her hand and you will find that her grip is firm; step inside and the tour should begin immediately, one of Isel's guides leading you through the Hall, the Great Chamber, the Oak Room and the Elizabethan Range, past faded panels, mullioned windows of cream sandstone, ancient oak doorways, arrow slits and original oils. You will see Matthias Read's portrait of Isel, the bedroom haunted by Ada Morville, monogrammed marquetry celebrating the marriage of (one of many) Wilfrid Lawsons and the wildlife photography of Margaret Austen-Leigh. At the end of your visit, standing in the Entrance Hall, copies of this book piled on the table behind you beside the biographies of Percy Kelly and May Moore, you may well concur with Lady Egremont; its owner does indeed appear to 'have the feel of the place'. Isel is part of her and she of Isel, for within the inventory of that ancient place are counted Mary Elizabeth Burkett and her long and remarkable life.

Postscript

Time doesn't slip by now – it positively gallops. Since 2000 I suddenly realised that I had become old. I hadn't even realised it when I was 'middle aged' but when I had to have an 80th birthday party in October 2004, it hit me with a vengeance.

During the last year of the second millennium I had decided to have the house restored – pele tower re-rendered and pointing done on the north face. The work seemed to last for ages and although negotiations with the architect began in 1999 the last builders and contractors didn't leave the place till 2006 – it was a great relief. The pele tower is now dry and fit to offer guests as a bedroom and the colour of pink, although not intended, cheers the outside up. The great benefit to me was that I learnt how to point; watching one or two painstaking builders showed me the knack of putting lime mortar into the crevices. I managed to do the inside of the Sunken Garden Walls during the summer of 2003 and found it quite a therapeutic exercise. The builders, who eventually caught me at it, helped by leaving some unused mortar behind every day after work and it was a new bond between a really co-operative workforce.

Most years I went abroad somewhere. In 2003 Linda Sloss (David's widow) and I spent two lovely weeks in Morocco – Fez and Marrakech. Rosemary and I joined the Cumberland and Westmorland Archaeological and Antiquarian Society for a trip to Malta in the autumn. In 2004 I had to give an address at the Felt Conference in Hungary and Istvan and Co gave me a wonderful welcome – felt has come a long way. Esmé Lowe and family introduced me to the magic of Ninfa and its birds in 2005. Liam McDowall and family had stayed at Isel and I went to them for a few days in Holland in 2005 and to their new house in 2006, combining it with visiting my Dutch felt maker Inge Evers and friends.

I was trying to give some activities up; in fact I was being forced to do so by well-meaning friends. The monthly playing of the church organ at a service, especially considering my inefficiency at it, was one thing to go in 2005. I concentrated on three main Societies of which I was President – the International Felt Association, Cumbrian Decorative & Fine Art Society (they had their fund-raising party at Isel) and the Romney Society; in fact I went to Venice with the latter in 2007. I tried to avoid giving talks although I did two of those three and a half hour marathons at Higham Hall, the second in 2003 on Schwitters which was a feat of engineering with Jenny Cowern and partner Raymond helping me with switches and plugs as I varied the participants' experiences. I also did, at a moment's notice, a felt talk in a yurt at 'Upfront' for a friend who could not come. Naturally my deep interest in painting linked me to exhibitions and it was great to go to the Romney Show in Liverpool Art Gallery, where I met Jimmy Corkhill of *Brookside* fame, much to the amusement of John Lee and David Cross, who had taken me there. There began to be regular Kurt Schwitters conferences in ever-increasing hope of buying the Merz Barn site, actually achieved in 2006. Lake District artists Donald Wilkinson and Julian Cooper both had successful shows at Dove Cottage.

I launched an Exhibition at Keswick Museum in its struggle to maintain itself when threatened with closure and helped to campaign for friends for it, and also for the Armitt Museum which has been in a threatened state from 2003. With the Old Friends of Abbot Hall we visited Andy Goldsworthy's studio and workshop in Scotland, and it was a poignant experience to go to Stranraer to see Jenny Cowern's last exhibition 'A Softer Landscape' – she was by that time very ill. I was persuaded to lend to, and open, an excellent exhibition to Howard Somervell at the Brewery Art Centre in 2006. I still kept on buying pictures and had acquired three nice Julian Coopers but missed the one I really wanted. It was wonderful to accompany Edward Hughes to Brantwood to see his 'service' on the dining table.

Also I kept firmly associated with the Cumbrian Wildlife Trust and managed to persuade Melvyn Bragg, David Bellamy, Sir Chris Bonnington and Eric Robson to address and lecture for the charity.

Castlegate House held a Sheila Fell show on 3 April 2005, to which her daughter Anna and two friends came. I was persuaded to join the Committee of Farfield Mill, Sedburgh, by Ann Pierson – very interesting and enjoyable. Also on the art front I became heavily involved in trying to help resuscitate Rosehill Theatre's classical music programme, in particular the music panel's objectives. Having been such a friend of the Sekers family it feels only right.

Not having a family of my own, and having very few close relatives, friends have always played a major role in my life. It is one of the hardest things to bear when they begin to die – to lose them at 100 or 96 is to be expected but it was still very sad when dear people such as Mollie Ponsonby (101), Margaret Fletcher (96 – last seen in March 2005), Clare Fell, May Moore, and Josefina de Vasconcellos died. There was also Jacquetta Lowther Bouch, and my last remaining aunt by marriage – Mary Burkett of Appleby, my father's brother's widow. We had fortunately had a special party for Josefina de Vasconcellos at Hutton in the Forest and I hadn't been able to attend the large one at Grasmere – it was overflowing owing to J de V adding a 'few names'.

But to lose younger friends is much harder. Jenny Cowern's illness for nearly a year was a tragedy and also Edward Hughes, who had been a friend, tenant and great potter, fell from Pillar to his death in a storm. Lorna Graves and David Nicholls died in 2005–6. I tried to carry out Jenny's wish to look after her mother at Hames Hall, till she too died in the spring of 2007.

Somehow life goes on. Healing nature is all around – though the red squirrel has left Isel and the greys are flooding in, despite all efforts of Red Squirrel Alert, on which I sit. I saw the last one here in 2005. The Blue Pheasant was away for several months and is now back and very faithful. I saw my first siskin at Isel on 20 April 2006. The ospreys returned in 2006 to Bassenthwaite – first the male and then the female right on schedule – followed by a flock of spectators.

The unwelcome side of the natural habitat is the recent spread of the weed Himalayan Balsam, brought over here in the early nineteenth century and now ever rapidly colonizing all our wetlands and river margins. It is particularly rife in the Lake District and wrecking special places such as Grasmere and Rydal and only recently have any efforts been tried by the authorities to try and curb it. Our river is one place affected, and when it shows in mid summer it is essential to pull it up before it makes its venomous seeds, which explode when ripe and spread the plant.

Cows invaded Mary's Wood, making deep foot-marks and spoiling the flat environment. Later sheep got in. Huge efforts were made to prevent another invasion of either. A much nicer task, and one which took nearly a year, was clearing a path along the side of the beck running west to east from the foot of the steps. This took work parties, the tree specialist and gardener many hours but it is a lovely new area which had lain covered with fallen trees for over fifty years.

The Larsen trap has kept the magpies down. To add to the joys of living in the Lake District, a visit to the Holker Garden Show is always a must on the last weekend of May. A visit with landscape artist Donald Wilkinson and wife Shirley to Little Sparta was very rewarding.

I try to go to the August birthday party for Tibetan monastery Samyling in Scotland when I can. There seemed to be more and more 80th birthdays; one was Jackie Barratt at Storr's Hall. The Konevets Russian Quartet made it to Greystoke in 2002 – they usually come to Isel. The Levens Concerts continue to be very happy occasions and well supported, and there were good lectures at Dove Cottage where David Wilson replaced Robert Woof – who died sadly. New friends like the Woodhouses came to live here bringing enthusiasm and interest in the area. The Senhouse Museum continued to flourish and actually was able to erect its Watch Tower, which commands a wonderful panoramic view right along the Solway. I heard in 2005 that Rosa Ottunbaeva (former Ambassador to Britain from Kyrgyzstan, who had come to Isel and met Jenny) was in the second line of the march in Bishkek when they had a recent uprising.

More people paid vast sums at charity auctions to try to 'visit' the Isel ghost but again 'she' wasn't playing and when the Burchetts came in June 2005 they left without seeing her.

The writing programme went on all the time. In 2002 the Cockermouth School of Painting – 'Sutton and his Circle' had a launch at High Rogerscale. It was lovely to meet again Nikolai Tolstoy whom I hadn't seen since he was 17. Nikolai had just finished writing the first book on Patrick O'Brian with whom, with his wife, I had a great friendship in the 1950s. It was fun to contribute some photos, letters and information towards the next book on Patrick. A book on Assassin Castles revealed that Girdkuh – which Genette and I had found in 1962 near Damghan, Northern Persia – had been revisited four years later. As we were the first westerners to climb it and report it, albeit in a small article in the *Times* in 1962, on our return we felt it was time to publish our diaries which we had written on our travels in 1962. John Murray was prepared to publish it then if we had had time to edit it. We hadn't – Genette had decided on which of her admirers to marry and was getting wed and I was starting at Abbot Hall on 5 November 1962. So some of my marvellous guides helped me proof-read and Genette did her share in Putney and *The Beckoning East* came out before Christmas 2006 and we gave them to old friends and people we had known before and during our trip to Turkey and Iran – just to put the record straight on the fact we found it in 1962.

I had been to London in the winter of 2006 and met a lot of my old Persian contacts. It was great fun to go to stay with a friend near Taunton in 2005 only to find when I got to the station that there had been a muddle over train times and I had forgotten the address and telephone number of my friend. But it all ended happily when Priscilla turned up to meet the train a little later.

My car had blown up in January 2005 and I was persuaded by the garage to change from Peugeots (I'd had the last for ten years) to a little silver Toyota – which has been very good so far.

In an old pupil's car I was taken down to Wroxall Abbey, where I had taught at the Laurels in the 1950s before coming up to Ambleside. It had been a delight to be with people who were then just embarking on their lives only now quite disturbing to find some of them have retired. Another reminder of my teaching days was when some old students took me out to lunch in 2006 – last seen forty-four years ago.

In 2006 it was great fun to participate in a film commentary on A Wainwright, whom I had known first in 1962. Flora Davies, Hunter's daughter, was in charge and a delightful film crew had me wandering round the Sunken Garden with shears and secateurs all morning, weeding, none of which showed on the excellent film they produced later. Coleridge scholar Mollie Lefebure was also featured and many people saw it.

In the autumn of 2006 my tenant in the flat and friend Nancy Tingey went back to her family in Australia and I missed her stimulating artistic input and many exhibitions. She used to work at Abbot Hall in the 1960s and came over here to take an MA at Carlisle and see her parents before they died.

One very enjoyable task we carried out in 2006 was done with the help of Leslie Greenbank and his wife on two stone collections in Cumbria. Leslie was a miner I had known in Kendal days and he agreed to look at and organise the stone collections at Dallam Tower and Fawe Park. Both owners were delighted and most interested to know intimately about their collections. Leslie Greenbank is a world authority on Lakeland and other minerals. We were relieved to be able to destroy all the rotting and dangerous elements and leave each collection in an orderly and documented state.

After Jenny's death Val Rickerby and I started trying to do justice to her work in a monograph. We spent a great deal of time in 2006 getting it ready in time for the Exhibition at Tullie House which opened to a large audience on Friday 2 March 2007.

The discovery of a portrait of Jane Austen's nephew at Isel caused us and Chawton House great excitement. It was found in my picture-store torn in half and through the kindness of David Selwyn from the Jane Austen Society it is being cleaned and restored and then lent to them for a period.

The Isel House owners came from New Zealand and we had a lovely tea with the guides with the Papps of Isel House, Nelson. Angela Locke was the connection as she had just been to New Zealand.

The Senhouse Museum poetry group which Angela Locke leads are going from strength to strength and members have won the Ottaker prize. Hugh Thomson won the Mirehouse Prize in 2006.

Three people in particular deserve thanks for having helped me with my share of the proofreading – Dorathy Morgan, Carol Vanessa Hudson and Joan Judt. I'd like to thank the author Ben Verinder for having the idea to write the book and persisting despite my prevarications. Finally my thanks to all the many friends whom he has brought into his account for they have enriched the various chapters of my life. There are too many for mention to have been made of everyone I have met but the others are not forgotten. Thanks go to Melvyn Bragg and Roy Strong for their kind words.

M E Burkett

Bibliography

Abbot Hall Art Gallery Catalogue, Abbot Hall Art Gallery and Museums, 1977.

Abbot Hall Art Gallery Director's Annual Report for 1973/4, Abbot Hall Art Gallery and Museums, 1974.

Alliluyeva, Svetlana, *Twenty Letters To A Friend*, Harper, 1967.

Bullock, Alan, *Hitler and Stalin: Parallel Lives*, Vintage Books, 1993.

Burkett, Mary E., *I Was Only A Maid*, Firpress Limited, 1998.

Burkett, Mary E., *John Bracken* (*monograph*), Abbot Hall Art Gallery and Museums, 1976.

Burkett, Mary E., *Kurt Schwitters – Creator of Merz*, Abbot Hall Art Gallery and Museums, 1979.

Burkett, Mary E., *The Art of the Felt Maker*, Abbot Hall Art Gallery, 1979.

Burkett, Mary E., *The Skiddaw Hermit*, Skiddaw Press, June 1996.

Burkett, Mary E., and Rickerby, Valerie M., *Percy Kelly – A Cumbrian Artist*, Skiddaw Press, 1997.

Burkett, Mary E., and Sloss, David, *Read's Point of View*, Skiddaw Press, 1995.

Coburn, Broughton, et al., *Everest: Mountain Without Mercy*, National Geographic Society, 1997.

Davies, Hunter, *Wainwright*, Michael Joseph, 1995.

Gaussen, Alice, *Men of the Midi*, Alexander Maclehose and Co., London, 1934.

King, Dean, *Patrick O'Brian: A Life Revealed*, Henry Holt and Company, 2000.

Lamborn Wilson, Peter, *Scandals: Essays in Islamic Heresy*, Autonomedia, 1995.

Mantovani, Roberto, et al., *Everest: The History of the Himalayan Giant*, Mountaineers Books, 1997.

Oxford University Press Web Site – Sir Hugh de Morville – Contributor W. H. H. Prial, Frank J., *New York Times*, 9 Oct. 1998, New York Times Internet Archive.

Radkinsky, Edvard, *Stalin: The First In-Depth Biography Based On Explosive New Documents From Russia's Secret Archives*, Hodder and Stoughton, 1996.

Roger of Pontigny in *Materials for Life of Becket*, iv. 73; Richard of Hexham, Chron. Stephen, &c., Rolls Ser. iii. 178.

Stark, Freya, *The Valley of the Assassins*, Methuen, 1934.

Stevenson, Joseph (translator), *The Church Historians of England*, volume V, part 1, pp. 329–336, London, Seeley's, 1853.

Index